For Richer, for Pc

For Richer, for Poorer

EARLY COLONIAL MARRIAGES

Edited by
Penny Russell

MELBOURNE UNIVERSITY PRESS
1994

First published 1994
Typeset by Syarikat Seng Teik Sdn. Bhd., Malaysia, in 11/13 Baskerville
Printed in Malaysia by SRM Production Services Sdn. Bhd. for
Melbourne University Press, Carlton, Victoria 3053
U.S.A. and Canada: International Specialized Book Services, Inc.,
5804 N.E. Hassalo Street, Portland, Oregon 97213-3644
United Kingdom and Europe: University College London Press,
Gover Street, London WC1E 6BT

This book is copyright. Apart from any fair dealing for the
purposes of private study, research, criticism or review, as
permitted under the Copyright Act, no part may be reproduced by
any process without written permission. Enquiries should be made
to the publisher.

© Melbourne University Press 1994

National Library of Australia Cataloguing-in-Publication entry

For richer, for poorer: early colonial marriages.

   Includes index.
   ISBN 0 522 84551 7.

   1. Marriage—Australia—History—19th century. 2. Upper
classes—Australia—History—19th century. 3. Australia—Social
life and customs—19th century. I. Russell, Penelope Ann.

306.810994

Contents

Preface	*ix*
Contributors	*xi*
Introduction	*1*
Authority and affection: John and Charlotte Bussell Marian Quartly	*12*
Lives in exile: Elizabeth and John Macarthur Hazel King	*31*
Paradise lost: Sir John and Lady Jane Franklin Penny Russell	*50*
A marriage of opposites: Charles Joseph and Sophie La Trobe Marguerite Hancock	*73*
The moral reformer and the imperial major: Caroline and Archibald Chisholm Patricia Grimshaw	*94*
The damned whore and the public man: Sarah and William Wentworth Carol Liston	*114*
Notes	*135*
Index	*143*

Illustrations

	page
John Garrett Bussell	15
Battye Library, Perth 4599B/59	
Charlotte Bussell	29
Battye Library, Perth 4599B/60	
Elizabeth Macarthur	34
From the original in the Dixson Galleries, State Library of New South Wales	
A sketch of the cottage, Camden, in 1834	38
Mitchell Library, State Library of New South Wales	
Elizabeth Farm, Parramatta, the home of John and Elizabeth Macarthur	44
Photograph by the author	
John Macarthur, *c.* 1817	48
From the original in the Dixson Galleries, State Library of New South Wales	
Jane Griffin, aged twenty-four	51
National Portrait Gallery, London	
Captain John Franklin, naval commander and explorer	55
Mitchell Library, Sydney	
Jane as Lady Franklin	60
Queen Victoria Museum and Art Gallery, Launceston	
Sir John Franklin	71
National Portrait Gallery, London	
Sophie La Trobe with her daughters, Eleanora and Cecile	80
Photograph, Joan Ritchie collection, State Library of Victoria	
'Jolimont, from the hill beyond the Yarra Yarra', 1854	82
State Library of Victoria	

viii Illustrations

'Front view of Jolimont' 85
State Library of Victoria
'View of the detached cottage, Jolimont' 90
State Library of Victoria
A detail from the *Morning Post*, 8 February 1854 92
Archibald Chisholm as a young officer in the 30th Madras
Native Infantry 97
Mr H. J. Chisholm, Sydney
A contemporary portrait of Caroline Chisholm 101
'A carol on Caroline Chisholm' 103
Punch, August 1853
Sarah Wentworth in the 1860s 119
Collection of the Historic Houses Trust of New South Wales
William Charles Wentworth in the 1880s 124
Collection of the Historic Houses Trust of New South Wales
Vaucluse House in the late 1870s 129
Wentworth Papers, Mitchell Library, Sydney
Entrance Hall, Vaucluse House, 1869 131
Dixson Library

Preface

When the idea for this book was suggested to me, I found the prospect of combining the discipline of history with the pleasure of romance irresistible. Evidence about personal relationships between married couples is rarely examined for its own sake outside biographies. The distribution of work, power and responsibility between the sexes has rightly begun to receive serious academic attention, but the impact of this upon the subjective patterning of the emotions is more difficult to determine. In this book the attempt to do so also offers a fresh perspective on early colonial society.

The task could not have been attempted without the basis of previous historical research to rest upon. Much good work has been done in publishing and interpreting the diaries and correspondence of individuals and couples, and piecing together more scattered evidence where such substantial personal material has not been available. All the articles in this volume reveal a debt to such earlier work, whether undertaken for a wider project by the contributor herself or published by another historian. The gradual increase in publishing of Australian material over the past few decades now makes a project of interpretation such as this not only viable but a pleasure.

We are grateful to Melbourne University Press for taking up this project, and I would like to record my particular acknowledgement of Venetia Nelson's careful work on the manuscript.

Every effort has been made to obtain permission to use copyright material; the publishers trust that their apologies will be accepted for any errors or omissions.

Penny Russell

Contributors

Patricia Grimshaw is an associate professor in history at the University of Melbourne where she specialises in women's history and women's studies. She is the author of *Women's Suffrage in New Zealand* and *Paths of Duty: American Missionary Wives in Nineteenth Century Hawaii* and is co-editor of several books including *Australian Women: Feminist Perspectives*, *The Half-Open Door* and *Families in Colonial Australia*.

Marguerite Hancock is presently completing a Master of Arts degree at the University of Melbourne. In 1985 she contributed a chapter on the life of Georgiana McCrae to Marilyn Lake and Farley Kelly (eds) *Double Time: Women in Victoria—150 Years* (1985). From 1985 she has worked at Government House, Melbourne, as secretary to the wife of the Governor of Victoria.

Hazel King is a Member of the Order of Australia and holds a D. Phil. from Oxford University. She was formerly a senior lecturer in History at the University of Sydney. She is a Fellow of the Royal Australian Historical Society and was its President in 1982-85. She has contributed numerous articles to the *Australian Dictionary of Biography* and to historical periodicals. Her published books include *Richard Bourke* (1971), *Elizabeth Macarthur and Her World* (1981), *One Woman at War: Letters of Olive King 1915-1920* (1986), and *Colonial Expatriates: Edward and John Macarthur Junior* (1989).

Carol Liston lectures in historical studies at the University of Western Sydney, Nepean. Her particular interests include nineteenth-century New South Wales, local history, biography and family history. The author of *Campbelltown: the Bicentennial History* (1988) and *Sarah Wentworth: Mistress of Vaucluse* (1988), she is at present researching a history of Parramatta and editing a collection of Suttor family letters. She was president of the Royal Australian Historical Society from 1988 to 1993 and is currently a vice-president.

Marian Quartly (formerly Aveling) teaches history at Monash University. She is interested mainly in the nineteenth century. Her publications include the co-authored *Australians 1838* (1987) and a forthcoming feminist short history of Australia. She is at present writing a book about gendered citizenship and the shape of the Australian state around 1900.

Penny Russell is a lecturer in Australian History at the University of Sydney. She is interested in representations of femininity, especially in relation to class, nationalism and imperialism. She is the author of '*A Wish of Distinction': Colonial Gentility and Femininity* (forthcoming), and is currently working on a thematic history of women in Australia.

Introduction

For Richer, For Poorer is the story of six colonial marriages. Six contributors trace patterns within marriages of partnership and power, work and companionship, affection and disenchantment. Together they demonstrate that marriages in the early nineteenth century, formed and lived under trying circumstances, could be as much about working together as about emotions and desire.

The partnerships were all 'colonial marriages': not simply because they occurred within Australia's early colonial period, but because their participants, male and female, were fundamentally caught up with the expansion of empire through conquest, colonisation and civilisation. The marriages were lived out not in Australia alone, but within a wider context of the empire: indeed, only one marriage ceremony out of the six was held in Australia, and only three out of the twelve marriage partners died in Australia. Yet it can be argued that the Australian experience was in each case crucial in establishing the character of the marriage. Choices about the relationship shaped and were shaped by various aims in colonisation: to conquer or to settle, to rule or to reform, to invest everything and build a new life in the colony, or to exploit it for wealth and social status with the aim, ultimately, of returning 'Home'.

The marriages described in this volume are those of men and women who believed they held a natural right to leadership in the colony. They are the marriages of the governors, the landowners, the lawyers, the philanthropists of the early colonies of Australia.

They cannot, therefore, be taken as representative of all marriages in the early colonial period. The difficulties these men and women suffered were isolation and adjustment to an alien environment, not poverty and oppression. These are, by and large, stories of success.

Little has been written about the marriages of these successful people. It may come as a surprise to some to learn that Caroline Chisholm had a husband at all, or that Charles Joseph La Trobe's wife was Swiss born. Despite a growing interest by historians in private life, the image of colonial society remains by and large one of conquest, settlement and penal servitude. There is another face to that history. The marriages of individuals had a lot to do with their attitudes to colonisation. A study of the marriages of the privileged classes can reveal much about the intersections of power and partnership.

The relationship between the concepts of marriage and colonisation, especially for those who regarded themselves as the natural leaders of the new society, was a curious one. They were at once inseparably linked and totally incompatible. Both, ideologically speaking, were about laying the foundations of a future society, and founding the ruling dynasties of that society. Both looked to a future created by the efforts of individuals in the present; and both rejoiced in the relationship thus established with posterity, hoping that their heirs would look back with gratitude and pride on their 'founding fathers' (or mothers). Both, then, shared assumptions about progress, advancement and future generations. Marriage was central to colonisation, because colonisation was about making families.

But at the same time the *idea* of colonisation acted to exclude marriage and domesticity altogether. To the colonists, 'Home' was England, while the colonies represented frontiers where men could be real men, testing their masculinity far from the stultifying impact of anxious wives and wailing children. Colonisation was expressed in terms of conquest, domination, the penetration of the interior, the building of a new society: images not only implying values and abilities deemed masculine in nineteenth-century society, but drawing, sometimes explicitly, on the language of male sexuality. In fact in the early nineteenth century one is more likely to find sexuality sublimated in colonialist discourse than present in personal writing about private relationships. Women had 'no place' in the concept of the colonised bush because the masculine/feminine dichotomy was set up between man the penetrator, the conqueror who wrested the fruits of his labours from a reluctant land, and the bush itself, wilful, reluctant, feminine, romanticised, requiring to be conquered or seduced before 'she' would yield up her riches. Thus two important elements in marriage—domesticity and sexuality—held their most powerful ideological place in the language of the relationship between England and the frontier, rather than in the private experience of marriage from which the metaphors were drawn.

Though women seemed to be excluded by this relationship between men and the land, the romantic language of colonisation or imperial expansion did in some respects inform relationships between the sexes. The concept of a romantic hero, loved, like Othello, 'for the dangers [he] had pass'd', was central. In a time when little allowance was made for female sexual desire, the dynamic of the Romantic ideal allowed women to articulate a fervent admiration for heroic masculinity. The masculine language of conquest became the feminine language of desire. And heroism, in that imperial age, was depicted in terms of exploration, conquest, and pioneering.

The foundation on which heroism rested varied considerably between individuals. During a startlingly brief courtship, the widowed Charlotte Cooksworthy 'would with a greedy ear devour up' John Bussell's accounts of his colonial experience (as an observer wrote, paraphrasing *Othello*)—suggesting that he brought a breath of romance to her English drawing-room. But not all her friends thought that John Bussell's status as a Western Australian colonist made him desirable. As a young girl, Sophie de Montmollin thrilled to the adventurous rambling spirit of her cousin's tutor, Charles La Trobe, only to find, when he became Superintendent of the Port Phillip District, that his restless spirit took him from her all too often. For Jane Griffin, the colonial experience must have represented some tarnishing of a romantic image. Marrying John Franklin after his triumphant return from a successful Arctic expedition, she found herself within a few years in Van Diemen's Land, her husband now harassed by daily administrative cares as Lieutenant-Governor, and needing energetic support—which she cheerfully gave him—rather than passive admiration for his heroism. Elizabeth Veale fell for a devil-may-care young military man, John Macarthur, whose quarrelsome and high-handed nature was to invest her marriage with constant nervous strain and long periods of separation, even after he left the army and turned to farming. In the other two marriages discussed here the image of romantic masculinity is more hazy. Resisting the allure of the military, Caroline Jones coolly demanded a bargain of Archibald Chisholm before she consented to marry him, determined that her marriage should help rather than hinder her vocation for philanthropy. William Wentworth had a different appeal. The brash 'native son', adventurous, vulgar and ambitious, possessed the charm of the colonial, not the romantic image of the coloniser.

If women's desire for men was expressed in terms of the romantic colonial ideal, were there complementary charms in the colonising woman? Othello loved Desdemona 'that she did pity [him]', but did colonising men seek in their wives only an enthusiastic and sympathetic audience for their exploits? The stories presented here suggest not. Only Sophie La Trobe remained in the role of passive admirer throughout her marriage, discouraged by illness, a barrier of language, caste and shyness, and her husband's ambiguous social position from carrying out active social duties as his wife. Jane Franklin, by contrast, though equally unenthused by social duties, travelled and explored by her husband's side and on her own, and became so interested in his administrative chores that both partners came under the scornful criticism of their colonial detractors: she for interfering in affairs of state, he for being 'under petticoat government'. Caroline Chisholm's reforming work increasingly took precedence in her and Archibald's lives, dictating their domestic arrangements and choice of living place. John Macarthur relied on Elizabeth, and John Bussell on Charlotte, to manage estates in their absence, and in the end, though both husbands kept up a hectoring tone in their letters and enquiries about the state of affairs, it appears that their wives may have had a better understanding of the business than they did themselves. Charlotte achieved this place by persistence, Elizabeth because she had no choice, but both women proved indispensable for their farming skills. Men may have been drawn to women who offered hero worship, but they expected their wives to possess practical skills which would materially improve the social and economic condition of the new family.

One marriage in this book defies all these generalisations. William Wentworth and Sarah Cox were both born in Australia, both were illegitimate and had at least one convict parent. William Wentworth occupied a privileged position in the colony only because his father, despite a dubious past, was a surgeon who could afford to educate his son as a gentleman. Wentworth could have looked higher for a wife, could have sought a partner who would enhance his social respectability. Instead he outraged colonial society by marrying his mistress. The basis for attraction here does not need to be understood in terms of a discourse of imperial romance. Between the rough but rising public man and the blacksmith's daughter earthy sexual desire was more openly avowed. This had serious implications for their relationship throughout their marriage. Sarah could never play a role in her husband's social success, the scandal of their belated marriage proving a sticking point in her, if not his, entry to society. The marriage depended on the continuation of sexual attraction, affection and companionship, never becoming an economic and social alliance.

Focusing on the marriages of celebrated people, this book necessarily attempts to move between public and private life. The difficulty of doing so appears strikingly when concentrated in a particular editorial dilemma: the problem of naming. Public names are not the same as private names—particularly in the nineteenth century, when boundaries between public and private were more rigid. Written sources, however apparently 'private', do not always answer the vexed question of how husband and wife addressed each other in bed, at the breakfast table, or in front of servants. In this book, writers' willingness to use surnames or first names reflects differing relationships between the historian and her subject. A major influence on this relationship is the nature of the sources themselves. Fresh from the perusal of the intimate diaries of the young Jane Griffin, I could happily think of her as 'Jane', except when she was engaged in political dealings. But for Marguerite Hancock, Sophie La Trobe's elusive identity remained that of the governor's wife, 'Mrs La Trobe'.

The problem of naming has a particular gender dimension. When history was only about men, and only about public life, the dilemma did not exist: men were referred to by surname alone. To continue this practice in a discussion of a marriage necessarily privileges the identity of the husband over that of the wife—what name is left for her that neither infantilises her nor emphasises her anonymous dependence? And yet the powerful public persona of men like 'La Trobe' and 'Wentworth' defies even the most intrepid historian's attempt to discover—let alone name—a more private and vulnerable individual.

These marriages suggest a colonial experience organised on gendered lines, but by no means inflexibly so. Though women had no share in the heroic mythology of conquest and colonisation, they did share in the hard work of pioneering and took an active interest in notions of civilisation. And if the marriages presented here are a guide, men, far from resenting their wives' presence or attempting to break loose from domestic constraints, welcomed, sought and indeed demanded their assistance. Imperial masculinity had a broader dimension than that implied in conquest alone. A domestic ideal of manliness, with an emphasis on moral rectitude, religious values, family and responsibility also had its place in colonial society. The two elements of masculinity were in constant tension—Franklin's escape to the polar wastes after the confining experience of colonial administration was the most obvious example—but this in itself indicated that there was not a simple masculine dominance in the arena of colonisation. Though lured by the romantic appeal of the colonial male, women created their own space and their own sense of purpose. The gendered engagement in colonisation was represented in terms of partnership.

The pressures of the colonising life itself tended to draw emphasis away from romance and the language of desire and place it instead upon the concept of a working partnership. Wilson Hardy, a colonist drawn by the lure of gold to attempt to make his way in Victoria in the 1850s, soon regarded a wife as an indispensable aid to his progress. He suggested to his sisters in England that the demand for wives far outstripped supply, with the result that physical attraction moved well down on the list of requirements in a bride. It was, he wrote, 'a never to be glutted market: it surrounds all, the halt, the red haired, oblique visioned, the toothless, the aged, the secondhand; in fact all may get married here; people haven't time to stick to scruples . . .'[1]

Among convicts and free immigrants alike, wealthy or poor, the desire for a partner who would assist in working towards economic and social advancement was regarded as a laudable reason for marriage. Affection was a desirable ingredient, but it was not necessary for it to be present before the marriage took place. When male convicts sought permission to marry they tended to emphasise their own industrious habits and to claim that they sought to advance themselves by taking wives whom they represented as 'good managers, good businesswomen and sometimes good mothers'. By these means, with the occasional reference to 'mutual affection', but none at all to the prospective wife as an object of passion or desire, the convicts hoped to appeal to the authorities. Where marriage was seen as the basis for moral reform and a stable civilised society, partnership in work and the rearing of families was envisaged, rather than romantic love.[2] Caroline Chisholm explicitly fostered these qualities of marriage for the improvement of men and society. The privileged classes themselves, though familiar with the literature and poetry which celebrated romantic love, rarely allowed passion to interfere with a marriage of mutual social benefit.

Wilson Hardy offered a satirical version of the new colonist's desire for a working partner, rather than a 'lady', for a wife. His letter to his sister continued:

> ... they are really so bad to get here I think I will just send you an order for one. I am not particular about the weight size or beauty so that she must be a good sound bouncing lass with *teeth* and character and refinement, a character of common sense and willing to off her artificials and go through thick and thin *should* it be required. Of course she would be gratified to knit, sew, wash, serve and cook in ordinary degree and does not matter if she never heard of a crotchet [*sic*] needle or saw a carpet. I am afraid I shall be too fastidious if I say any more; in short I might have said a good stout country lass would do me—a genteel finical lady wont do now you understand.[3]

Whereas in England social advancement might be sought, or consolidated, through the selection of a marriage partner of a higher social status, in the more fluid society of the colonies it would be achieved through husband and wife working together. But the disregard for birth and breeding was never total—even when in a bantering humour, Wilson Hardy placed 'character and refinement' right after his demand for teeth as a basic requisite in a wife. Even this degree of indifference to social standing did not survive the advance to prosperity, whether in individuals or in the colony as a whole. In the heady days of convict Sydney, William Charles Wentworth could marry his mistress. But in a society becoming ever more settled, prosperous, and conscious of social caste, such a marriage carried significant social penalties, which Sarah felt rather more than did her husband. The transition was similar to that which occurred on an individual level across classes and throughout the colonial period. By the time Wilson Hardy did marry, he was more established in life, and his vision of a 'bouncing country lass' gave way to a more romantic, and status-conscious, ideal in the woman he finally chose for his wife:

> That I have quite made up my mind to get married is certain, but when, I cannot tell—as she is so very young and I have to wait perhaps a year or two as she is but 19 and very inexperienced—knowing nothing of the world—you may believe she is a 'proper' girl when I tell you I have waited a year or two and will probably have another to wait—one that has a *head and a heart* and whatever else is wanting may be acquired—she is a lady by education and is beloved by all who know her so that I am sure my sisters would love her as dearly as I do—her appearance is not so prepossessing as her natural disposition and though not brought up to the duties of domestic life she is naturally not incapable of filling them ... However Lizzie she is a '*prize*' and makes a great sacrifice to me—for my physical wreck and moral inferiority makes me totally unworthy of such a girl.[4]

Love, clearly, could precipitate a considerable readjustment of ideas, and disrupt calculations of future benefit. But even romantic love, with which this passage is imbued, did not totally eliminate consideration of particular advantages. Polly Hardy was not trained in domestic duties, but she would not therefore be spared the necessity of assuming them. The romantic image of femininity, indeed, may well have been of a lady through and through who could miraculously acquire feminine domestic skills whenever called upon to do so.

Among the many papers of a New South Wales colonial family, the Scotts, is a collection of poems, neatly transcribed by hand in an exercise book which bears the name 'Mrs Mitchell' on the cover. One of Mrs Mitchell's poems (probably written by herself) was titled 'Supposed to be spoken by an Emigrant family in N.S.W.'[5] The chief sentiment expressed was grief at living a life away from the emotional centre of the family.

> *Our* harps that once so sweetly rung
> In pleasant days of yore,
> Now lie with silent chords unstrung
> Upon a foreign shore.

She lamented the severing of emotional links built through years of familiarity.

> The ties that bound us then, at first
> From earliest childhood grew
> And now that those old links are burst
> Our hearts are breaking too!

Yet in the later stanzas of the poem she looked forward with optimism to forming new attachments, new ties, with 'those who share our fate, / Our exile and its pain'. The last stanza is a celebration of the colonial family:

> A Mother's arms, a sister's kiss
> A father's smile, invite
> We'll drown in scenes of present bliss
> The thoughts of past delight.
> And as with brightened looks we gaze
> On each accustomed face
> The home we knew in other days
> We'll find in their embrace!

Separation and loss were integral to the experience of colonial wives: separation from family and loved ones, from 'Home', from female companionship, even from children. Women tended to become colonists because they had chosen to marry a particular man rather than because they embraced emigration for its own sake, so for them a 'colonial marriage' had a particular significance. Their husbands would have been colonists, married or not, and indeed the existence of a wife probably made the colonial condition more pleasant. Men were colonists as men and also as husbands. Women, with a few striking exceptions, were colonists as wives only.

Nineteenth-century marriage demanded an unquestioning transference of loyalty from the parental family to the husband. If that meant leaving home—which for thousands of women it did, and for some within days of marrying—women adjusted their sights accordingly, and turned their faces towards the future and new horizons. Their job was to create 'home' anew: both physically and emotionally.

They did so uncomplainingly, but as Mrs Mitchell's poem shows, they did not do so without some tugs at the heart-strings. The world of female relationships in the nineteenth century tended to be overshadowed by the public importance attached to marriage, but attachments to the parental family, siblings and friends were strong and lasting. The pain associated with separation was very real. Any marriage would create some disruption to these ties, but the disruption was greatly magnified if the husband announced his intention of heading for the colonies. Separated at one stroke from mother, sisters, aunt, friends, a colonial wife might have little prospect of ever seeing any of them again.

In such circumstances, marriage became not just a dominant but an all-determining relationship, imbued with a particular significance. Since it caused a total redefinition of all emotional relationships, it necessarily assumed enormous psychic significance in women's lives: women had much invested in the success of the partnership, in the companionship the marriage provided, and in the status which accrued to them through it, because they lost their former identities by marrying.

In the colonial context marriage had its own stresses. Economic reverses, administrative burdens, disappointments and hard work could all take their toll of a relationship. So, too, could the many separations associated with marriage in the colonies. John Macarthur's frequent and lengthy returns to England, the Wentworths' restless wanderings across the globe, John Bussell's teaching duties in Perth, Archibald Chisholm's military duties, Jane Franklin's explorations and travels and Charles La Trobe's adventurous treks around Port Phillip all meant that separations, of varying duration, were an integral part of the marriages presented here. For some women, and some men, this represented periods of freedom, for others periods of grief and anxiety.

Separation from children, too, was common: a phenomenon linked more with class position than with the colonial experience itself. Though childbearing, and lots of it, was an integral part of married life for most women, the definition of a good mother or a caring parent did not consist in the determination to keep children close in the domestic home. The demands of education, social training and even health often were felt as compelling reasons why parents should give up their children for considerable periods. All the parents discussed in this book underwent prolonged separation from beloved children. All felt this as a great grief, but only Sarah Wentworth expressed any feeling of remorse or sense that she had failed in her maternal duties.

The emphasis was not wholly on an intense personal relationship between wife and husband. Wealthy colonists tended to occupy large houses, with many people in them: immediate and extended family, guests, governesses, servants. The social and public existence of these individuals played an important part in their marriage relationship: the marriage was lived in and through that public identity, not separated out from it as haven and refuge.

Under such conditions, women kept up much of the important work of maintaining family links. They kept up a voluminous correspondence, exchanging family news and pictures, creating for the small colonial family a sense of attachment to England, and the larger family circle there. Responsible for creating 'home' in the colonies, they did so as much through writing as through action, maintaining a discourse of family in the face of absences and separations. 'Home' was the domestic environment, the family, and England. It was the world left behind, and the world to be created. The colonial marriage was integral to both of those worlds.

Authority and affection: John and Charlotte Bussell

Marian Quartly

Early in November 1832, John Bussell in western Australia replied to a letter from the woman he loved, back in England. He began by recreating the scene around him.[1]

> It is now evening. I am many miles from any civilised habitation in the depths of an unmeasured forest; my attendants are preparing for me a screen of boughs to keep off the wind. I am seated by some rapids on an unknown river . . . The rest of the party, fatigued with unwonted exertion, have not yet raised themselves from the reclining posture which they adopted at their first halting. I suffer little inconvenience for I am now an old bushranger. The moon, a small crescent, begins to assume a yellow tinge . . . [the smoking fire] will presently burst into flame and yield the light that the fading orbs of Heaven deny . . .

The self-conscious drama continues through narrative, verse, argument and impassioned introspection. John explains that he must write in moments snatched from his duties as a leader of men. The same boat that brought his beloved's letter carried an official request. John was asked to lead a party to explore new pastures, some 50 miles through heavy redwood forest from the family's isolated holdings at Augusta, on the south-western tip of the continent. 'My leisure on this march', he writes, 'is devoted to you'.

John presents two self-images here for his beloved's approval. Before the call to the wild he appears as 'the Philosopher', sitting reading in 'my own private cot, or library, or cell, or study, or magazine, or bed-chamber'. When the boat approaches he dismisses 'for the night the Empress Theodora, Justinian, Belisarius and

Antonia', for he was reading Gibbon's *Decline and Fall of the Roman Empire*. He describes his 'cot'—or cottage—as a centre of civilisation, 'with its glazed windows (a luxury here), looking on the fairest prospect, its mantelpiece looking-glass, its blazing hearth, its dressing and writing table, its well-stored bookshelves of my own fabric[ation], its pictures of well-remembered objects . . .'.

But the room is equally a magazine, or ammunition store, and 'the gun, the rifle, the pistols, the bugle, the powder-horn, the shot-belt and the packets of cartridges ranged about, proclaim too clearly the prevalence of the law of force, and the necessity of the means of defence'. John also pictures himself as 'the colonist',

> a man perhaps of gentle habits, information, address, and family, stalking through the woods with his well-greased boots, his trowsers of canvas, his shirt of duck, his cap of fur, his faithful provider and protector, his gun, on his shoulder, his dog by his side . . .

Dogs and guns were vital to the colonists' economy, providing them with most of the meat in their diet. John's verse describing the journey remarks that

> If water there our search reward,
> Our weary limbs shall rest;
> The turf shall be the genial board,
> The chase supplies a feast.

But 'the law of force' opposed the colonist to man as well as beast. The verse notes that loaded guns and watching dogs stand guard against the 'lurking savage'. Manliness in western Australia required the will to shoot any Aborigines prepared to defend their land from invasion.

What called forth this display of romantic—if slightly ironic—heroism? What does his distant correspondent have to do, John asks, 'with Mr. Bussell's picknick parties? What relation can they have to any misunderstanding that may, or may not, have subsisted between us?'.

The fact was that she had rejected him. Her letter was written to inform him that she could not hold to the informal agreement that had existed between them since John and three of his brothers had left England in 1829. She was concerned about her role within the Bussell family: about her position in the household vis-à-vis his formidable mother; and about John's management of her not inconsiderable fortune, which she feared would be in the family's interests. She feared that he did not love her enough to put her interests first.

John deals briefly with her specific concerns. 'In domestic affairs, in her own circle my mother must be paramount', but 'a distinct household establishment' would save his bride from 'submitting to a secondary place in her husband's house'. The family's possessions must be jointly held, with John as 'the principal director', but she would not be impoverished; 'your income here would have been not merely a competency, but affluence'. He brusquely dismisses her wider fears; of course he loves her: 'could you have thought I would have dealt ungenerously with *you*? One likes a little confidence'.

John's strongest strategy is not to argue. Rather he presents himself as irresistibly heroic, one whose love any woman would be proud to claim.

> I hope and think you will be pleased to learn that the man on whose affections you made such impression, and who, you say, excited such interest in your own heart, instead of proceeding with piteous whinings, humiliating despondency or dastardly accusations to avert you from your purpose, has commenced with vigour and activity to bear the communications of your letter.

By the end of his letter he is bearing his rejection with a stoic resignation that must have brought tears to his reader's eye. 'I once indeed thought that [my happiness] ought to have been increased by a union with you.' Now he knows that it 'depends on no mortal'. Feeling himself 'an old young man', he exclaims 'with the Vandal king as he followed the triumph of his conqueror "Vanity, Vanity, all is vanity"'. He concludes with another of his poems:

> Tho' the halls of the wealthy no more shall invite me
> To join in their revels, or feast at their board,
> Tho' the soft strains of music no longer delight me,
> Though I'm spoiled of whate'er the gay world can afford,
> Though rarely society's voice can deliver
> My soul from its thoughts, my abode from its gloom
> Where the depths of the wood, and the still rolling river
> Afford me the spot where I've chosen a home,
> Yet do I repine not; the calms of reflection
> Have soothed the wild tumults that once tossed my breast,
> The past I regret not, nor shun recollection
> Of pleasures once followed, of pains once possessed.
> Farewell.
> J. G. Bussell.

Could anyone reject such nobility? The engagement was renewed. In 1926 the Bussells' biographer, Edward Shann, wrote of this letter that 'the Byronic self consciousness is a little too heavy for modern liking, perhaps'.[2] In these post-modern times, readers may be more appreciative of the Victorians' capacity 'to observe, convey and even relish the action of their most anguished emotions'.[3]

The image that John Bussell presents of himself as colonist and man of action arose readily out of the reading matter of John Bussell,

John Garrett Bussell

philosopher. John completed a gentleman's education in the classics at Oxford. He intended taking ordination as a clergyman of the Church of England, but instead was persuaded by his mother to lead his brothers to invest and multiply the family's meagre fortune in Swan River Colony. Books had a treasured place in the colonists' baggage. When their house went up in flames in 1833, 'the Encyclopaedias' were the first things saved, and 'the Bibles and the Byron' soon after.[4] English historians have noticed the appeal of Lord Byron's passionate poetry to 'serious Christians' in England, despite the poet's atheism and personal immorality; they note the similar intensity in religious and in romantic sensibility.[5] John Bussell had on hand fine models for his stoicism and independence in the Greek and Roman authors who filled his library, and excellent expressions of 'manly emotion' both in the Romantic poets like Byron, Gray and Wordsworth, and in theological authors like Paley.[6]

Bussell's background also prepared him to play the colonist as hero. Though the early death of their clergyman father left the Bussells dependent on the charity of friends and relatives, Mrs Frances Bussell managed to rear her children in the style of the gentry, the landowning class in England. Daughters learnt to recognise and reproduce an aristocratic 'selectness and refinement'[7] of dress and domesticity, and genteel poverty taught them the skills that supported such elegance. Sons became expert in the energetic field sports—shooting, hunting, fishing—that filled a country gentleman's day. John and his brothers brought their favourite dogs with them to Western Australia.[8] Inclination as much as necessity soon made John Bussell 'an old bushranger'.

The historians Davidoff and Hall discover in these decades a new style of masculinity in England—'the Christian middle class man'. Men who remade themselves in the style of 'Evangelical manhood' were pious and passionate, morally upright, restrained in everything but their domestic and religious commitment. They were men of power, but their strength was mental and moral—exercised as 'influence'—rather than physical. They were dedicated to the virtues of hard work, but followed intellectual, professional or business pursuits; the ideal was the clergyman. Davidoff and Hall see the new middle-class gentleman as consciously differentiating himself from an older style of manhood more appropriate for landowners and soldiers. 'Masculine nature, in gentry terms, was based on sport and codes of honour derived from military prowess, finding expression in riding, drinking and "wenching"[9]—and, one could add, in a life of absolute leisure supported by other men's labour.

John Bussell fits the model of the new masculinity in many ways. He was a faithful lover and became a faithful husband and father. He was and remained a deeply committed Christian, fulfilling all but the sacramental duties of a clergyman in his community.[10] His manner was serious, dignified; he inspired confidence in family and strangers alike. At 5 foot 6 inches in height he was not a tall man; a photograph taken in old age suggests pleasant features rather than commandingly handsome ones. But this colonial Christian gentleman did not reject all of the gentry model of masculinity; indeed, in migrating to Swan River Colony John Bussell was consciously pursuing the life of a landowning gentleman.

Historians have suggested that families who became large landowners in the Australian colonies—the 'colonial gentry'—were rarely secure in their gentry status at Home.[11] Membership of the English gentry was determined in the first instance by birth. In theory it was limited to aristocratic landowning families and their relatives, usually professional people involved with the armed forces, the law, and the Church of England. In practice impoverished families often found it impossible to maintain gentry lifestyle and gentry connections, and newly rich families from outside the gentry sometimes found it possible to buy land (or wives or husbands) and thus to qualify for membership. Both aspiring and declining gentry looked to the colonies as an easy source of land and gentry status.

Western Australia was especially attractive to those intent on creating a colonial gentry. For every £3 worth of capital invested in the colony settlers were entitled to 40 acres of land, whether the capital be in the form of goods, livestock or people; a servant brought into Swan River Colony earned his or her employer 200 acres of land.[12] The Bussells' stock of capital was not large, entitling them to a land grant of only 5500 acres. It included, among the pigs and fowls and hunting dogs, only one servant, and he was an old man valued more for his experience than his strength. Unlike most of his literate fellows, John Bussell intended to earn a manly independence by his own labour. In this he imitates neither Davidoff's middle-class, 'sedentary' gentleman, nor the leisured country gentleman of aristocratic tastes; rather he seems to look back to an older model of yeoman householder, 'whom possession of property had made independent and capable of having dependents'.[13]

The Bussells' gentility was never in doubt, neither to themselves nor to others of their class. Even travelling steerage the brothers were so clearly men 'of gentle habits, information, address and family' that ladies travelling cabin class offered conversation and games of chess. In the colony gentlemen offered advice, captains lent their sailors' services, and the governor gave free passage on the government boat and later a government salary. The family's sense of superiority is caught in John's report on the thirty or so people co-resident with the Bussells at Augusta: 'The society here is confined but good. Captain Molloy of the Rifles, and spouse, with ourselves, constitute the gentle settlers . . . .'.[14]

All the elements of John Bussell's self-dramatisation seem to have been confirmed and validated in the colonial setting. His role as leader of men (and women) was to a degree thrust upon him by the needs of his family. When the four Bussell brothers sailed to Swan River in 1829, John was twenty-six and his siblings nineteen, sixteen, and fourteen. John made all the major decisions, organised all joint activities, taught all three what he knew of practical pioneering, and 'tutored' the two youngest in academic studies in the evenings.[15] Observers reported that 'the deference paid to John by his younger brothers and their friends in general was no less remarkable than deserved'.[16] His sisters eagerly cast him in the role of head of the family; Fanny wrote that an acquaintance in Perth 'speaks of John just as people used to speak of Papa, dearest Mother. I can only pray that we may be equally worthy of him and you . . . .'.[17] After Mrs Bussell had arrived in the colony, Fanny wrote that 'John is a great solace to Mamma, who seems to depend upon him almost as she did on Papa in every affliction or trouble'.[18] John himself had a clear view of one source of his authority: 'If I appear to govern, it is by watching the inclinations of others and making it my study to avert rather than thwart what I may disapprove'.[19]

John's dealings with other settlers also tended to cast him as leader. The family's resources far exceeded those of the craftsmen, labourers and soldiers who settled nearby, and their establishment became a source of imported goods, breeding stock, wage labour and loans. Every Sunday John read liturgy and sermon to the collected community in his sitting room.[20] He gladly accepted the gentlemen's burden of supporting his social inferiors—though he preferred to see the relationship in terms not of social status but superior moral character. Writing to a clergyman friend of his labours in netting fish to feed the settlement in a time of famine, John describes the willing help he received from soldiers stationed there. He remarks with becoming modesty: 'It is surprising the attachment these fellows have shown for me and mine so different are we from the characters they have been taught to look up to in their gay and fashionable officers . . . .'.[21]

John Bussell's picture of himself as a man unlike other men was confirmed by those around him. His self-portrait as the colonist 'stalking through the woods' is nicely mirrored in his sister Fanny's account of his appearance on her arrival in the colony in 1833: 'rather barbarous, but quite poetical, in large canvas trousers made by his own hands, a broad leather belt, hair and beard both long, somewhat, and moustaches enough to give a bandit look.' She tells her mother that he 'has made a vow not to shave his beard until you come out, but he keeps it beautifully combed'.[22] Clearly colonial circumstance allowed—required—John Bussell to combine an ideal of romanticised self-sufficiency with his family's tradition of, in Shann's terms, 'evangelical gentility',[23] producing a sort of radical Tory version of the new masculinity.

In 1837 John returned to England to claim his intended, Miss Sophie Haywood. Probably he went without his beard and bandit moustaches. By this date the family was resettled at the Vasse, on the fertile plains which John had explored while wooing his beloved by letter. The blossoming there of gardens, poultry and livestock brought real prosperity to the family, and encouraged John to ask Sophie to share his life. Miss Haywood, the orphaned daughter of a West Indian planter, had grown up with the Bussell children, and John's sisters and brothers looked forward to his return with 'an affectionate and amiable wife in our dear Sophia'.[24] It was not to be.

John's stay in England began with 'affliction, sickness, and disappointment'.[25] The first was the death through consumption of a cousin, Capel Carter. She had been the family's chief link with England, the recipient of most of the letters Home, the supplier (and often the donor) of goods sent, and John's 'oldest and dearest friend'. In accepting her offer to pay his passage back to England, John had written: 'There is no one on earth to whom I would so willingly owe an obligation as to yourself'.[26] Capel was deeply religious, and John's religious support; she set him reading Paley's *Moral Philosophy*, and gathered the funds to erect a church at Busselton on the Vasse. She was also angelically beautiful, a picture in Shann's words of 'rare unearthly brightness'.[27] Here was a model of female beauty, generosity and wisdom which any wife would be struggling to match.

Sophie Haywood failed to do so. John wrote to his mother in March 1838 that the affair 'is at an end. We have had nothing but difficulties since my arrival'. His feelings for Sophie had been estranged by her 'foolish jealousy of my affections for you', and by her concern at the prospect of him controlling her property. He wrote: 'I have encountered distracting and humiliating scenes, and bear with her silly friends the character of a fortune hunter'. Things were patched up, but after a date had been set for the marriage John's health collapsed, and he wrote 'soliciting his freedom in plain terms'.[28] She replied, 'You are free'.[29]

John fled to the home of John and Emily Bowker in Plymouth. Emily was his aunt, his father's sister. There in July 1838 he met Charlotte Cooksworthy, also a relative of the Bowkers and a widow with three surviving children. Within three weeks they were engaged, and on August 22 they married. Charlotte was born in 1808, four years after John, and named for Queen Charlotte—sign then of a Tory allegiance. Her father was a naval officer, frequently at sea, and she and her brothers and sister were reared by a stepmother. At twenty she married; at thirty she had borne four children and lost one and a husband.

One of Mrs Frances Bussell's sisters wrote excitedly from Plymouth with news of this 'strangely sudden and unlooked for marriage'. It would, she trusted, 'promise more of happiness to both than such hasty steps generally lead us to hope'. Mrs Bussell was reminded that she had known Charlotte before her marriage. 'She was too pretty and interesting to be easily forgotten'; tall and very slight, 'dark hair and eyebrows with sweetly expressive blue eyes well fringed', a fair complexion, 'her figure wants roundness for perfection but the *tout ensemble* always pleases'. She combined 'a quiet composed and ladylike air with an affectionate manner'. The Plymouth relatives had some doubts about her practical 'qualifications for colonial life', but trusted to the example her sisters-in-law would set, to Charlotte's 'devoted love' and to her 'very high sense of duty'.[30] Here was an example of ideal femininity—restrained, ladylike, affectionate, devoted, dutiful, and by implication domestic —the female pair to the new Christian gentleman.[31]

Charlotte was probably attracted less to John's evangelical qualities than to his stance as the romantic colonial. An unnamed source describes how a mutual cousin questioned John in the Bowker drawing-room about his adventures in Swan River, and 'like Desdemona, Charlotte would with a greedy ear devour up his discourse and loved him for the dangers he had passed through'.[32] At the Haywoods John the colonist had been ridiculed; here he was endorsed.

Charlotte's own adventures to date had been religious. Before her husband's death in 1835, the couple had left the Anglican congregation and begun attending meetings at the Providence Chapel. The meetings followed the principles of a sect recently begun in Ireland, and later known as the Plymouth Brethren. The group promised the excitement of new knowledge, or of old knowledge newly discovered, in the form of prophecy and direct access to the mind of God. Its first adherents were professional men—clergymen, lawyers, army officers—plus the odd Lord and Lady. The Bible was believed to be 'an infallible and living book', Christ 'a living saviour' whose return was near, Heaven and Hell very present realities. Literature endangered the soul, especially romantic literature. Social and political reforms were 'but the whitewashing of a house built on sand'; a Christian's duty was 'not to save the world but to save people out of it'. Services in Plymouth were confined to prayers, praise and teaching led by those male members of the congregation who felt themselves chosen by God. Unlike more humble groups like the Primitive Methodists, Brethren congregations did not permit women to speak in the assembly.[33]

By John's report, Charlotte's enthusiasm for the Chapel was cooling before they met, and she had been guilty 'of going to [the Anglican] church once or twice, to the scandal of these celestial monopolisers'. On their engagement John bluntly refused an invitation to 'convert' to the sect, and 'you will not wonder', he wrote, 'that all threats, maledictions, excommunications were denounced upon the stray sheep that dared to love a wolf'.[34] Worse, the legal guardians of Charlotte's children were leading members of the Chapel, and they threatened to deny her custody if she married John. The couple solved the problem by kidnapping the children. With the help of the Bowker family the children were secretly brought on board the ship in which the Bussells were embarked for Australia, and stolen away before the guardians learnt of their going.

John seems to have been the manager of this affair, and Charlotte the nervous accomplice. She wrote of her fears after they had sailed, when it seemed that storms would make the ship put back to England:[35]

> This frightened me when dear John told me of it, almost out my life, and I felt that I would face any danger, any suffering than those whose hearts seemed more merciless than any storm could possibly be, for I doubted not someone would be at Falmouth ... to take my darlings from me; their anxiety, dear little things, was nearly as great as my own and their sleep had been troubled by dreams of boats full of guardians following them.

John continued to play the hero, though not without irony. He describes himself supporting his new family through storm and seasickness. 'Wife, children, servants all involved in the same helplessness, making beds and other ungrateful actions of children's maid and housemaid all devolved in a body on my devoted head.' The anti-romantic climax came when a wave broke into the ship 'washing wifey, dear wifey out of bed'.[36]

> Tho' I was most egregiously troubled I could not for the life of me help laughing at the absurd figure she cut with mouth open, gasping for breath and almost in a pet with the genius of the storm. Fortunately I was endowed with the patience of Job (tho' Charlotte denies this) ...

By the end of their travels Charlotte was used to such misadventures. She wrote a long letter Home describing their 36-hour passage from Perth to the Vasse in a tiny open boat, more than twelve hours of which were spent tossing at anchor off the coast in a 'dreadful gale'. Charlotte records the terror of a fellow passenger at the size of the waves, 'which were frightful to behold'. But she made a good breakfast of eggs and ship's tea.

On landing, their homecoming was delayed while John sent a messenger up to the house announcing their arrival *and* their marriage; they had travelled faster than the English mail and John had forgotten to post a letter from Perth. An awkward scene followed at the house when Mrs Bussell, unwilling to let John out of her sight, left Charlotte alone to introduce herself to her new brothers-in-law. But she kept smiling and eventually everyone was 'most kind'.[37]

Charlotte made it a habit to keep smiling. In that first letter she apologised for taking so long to write; 'the depressions into which I every now and then fall throw me back sadly'. If her later letters are invariably cheerful, it was because she took a firm decision that 'little worries' were only aggravated 'by writing, and talking to others, for nobody can help you to bear them but yourselves'. Much later in life she told her grandchildren not to write her sad letters. She told them that when faced by '*hard times*' at their property 'Cattle Chosen':[38]

> to get through it all I was enabled to maintain so happy a state of mind that, when my dear sister wrote to me in one of her letters from England, she made this remark—'you always write such happy cheerful letters dear Charlotte that they make me feel very happy about you . . .'

Her first battle was to introduce herself into the family as someone more than John's wife. It was a battle she may never have felt she won. Her very cheerful letters suggest that she set out to make herself indispensable to the family, a strategy that placed her in competition with her new sisters to be of service to her new brothers.

Mrs Bussell—'our dear little mother' in Charlotte's first letter from Cattle Chosen—was never the problem that Sophie Haywood had feared. Before Charlotte's arrival she had ceded the household management to her daughters—or more precisely the household labour. The Bussell women never made a virtue of manual labour as thoroughly as their men did in the early days; their image of femininity always included a servant or two to do the heavy household work, and most of the time they managed to find one, however unsatisfactory. But still they had to work much harder than women of their class in England, and at tasks considered more unpleasant. The three sisters took between them 'the three departments, Cook, Housemaid, and Chambermaid', and changed them every month. Fanny described how as chambermaid she went[39]

> to the different rooms of the boys to make their beds, look for their fleas, which we are gradually exterminating, and make their little dwellings look as comfortable as possible, for which she is rewarded by a pat on the shoulder in the evening, and the epithet 'a most admirable old girl' . . .

—an exchange suggesting both parties' unease at the need for such demeaning services.

Like other settlers in Western Australia, the Bussells resolved the problem that 'ladies did not work' by declaring that colonial ladies did, without any loss of social status. In their first days in Perth Fanny noted that 'selectness and refinement are more prevalent than in England. Yet no one scruples to assist in the duties of the "menage"'.[40] At Augusta their neighbour Mrs Molloy provided a model of genteel colonial behaviour: 'She is perfectly ladylike, and yet does not disdain the minutiae of domestic economy, an indispensable accomplishment in a settler's wife . . .'.[41]

Charlotte embraced the colonial model with enthusiasm. It was not only because of her height that her (rather short) mother-in-law christened her 'Tall Biddy', 'from her striking resemblance to a little picture in a nursery book she had when all were children at the Vicarage. "B for Tall Biddy, who made the puff paste . . . with sugar and lemon peel, quite to your taste"'.[42] Charlotte claimed—and 'almost immediately' was given—'the office of housekeeper'.[43] In July 1840 she wrote to Emily Bowker with an emphasis suggesting some exaggeration of the truth:[44]

> Dearest Aunt for your comfort I must tell you for I well know how anxious you are about me, that all my dear brothers here and sisters, with my dear little mother, seem thoroughly pleased and satisfied with my exertions to make home comfortable, for I am regularly installed as its Mistress and am honoured by the appellation of 'Missis' from the cook who receives no orders from anyone but myself. We each know our own work and never interfere with one another. I reign as supremely Mistress here, as Queen Victoria on her throne—no one finds fault with any arrangement I may think it wise to make or any order I give but on the contrary, frequently overwhelm me with praises.

The household journal, kept by Fanny Bussell at this period, is open to a different reading, with more stress on the mutual allocation of tasks. A typical entry reads:[45]

> 10th Wednesday. Fanny and Mrs. Macdermott folding. The native, Onion, arrived from Augusta, with a hammer from Mr. Turner for John. Fanny made some rearrangements upstairs. Dawson and Lawrence draining. Vernon hoeing turnips. The beer tapped. John and Charlotte washing.

Another report from outside the family suggests neither comfort nor order. In 1842 a visiting clergyman was impressed with the Bussells' dedication to the church, and found Charlotte an agreeable, unaffected woman who 'improves on acquaintance'.[46] He reported that at Cattle Chosen he got 'plenty of good feed'; 'they live however in a sad, dirty muddle and do not make themselves, considering their means, half so comfortable as they might'.[47]

By late 1840 John had finished building what was always called 'Charlotte's house'—in fact a large single-roomed hut at a little distance from the other dwellings—which served as John and Charlotte's bedroom and Charlotte's sitting room. In a letter to England, Charlotte delighted in its furnishings, 'so comfortable and so English-like'. She describes how John is particularly pleased with his washstand, remarking almost every day on its convenience; 'for it holds everything he requires so nicely and which on opening he can *see* at *one glance.* You know how the Bussells hate the trouble of *searching* for anything even for a moment . . .'. Charlotte likes her cosy fireplace, where she can cook breakfast for her 'dear brothers' when they are 'anxious to get the meal earlier than the usual family one'. 'Sometimes when a few of us are inclined for a cosy chat and tea quietly together, John and myself with Charley, Vernon and Alfred drink tea here and if either of them happens to be indisposed I am invariably favoured with a visitor for the whole day'.[48]

But little came of Charlotte's efforts to put herself at the emotional centre of family life. The unity of the group was already under strain when she arrived, with sisters marrying and brothers anxious to do the same. Probably Charlotte's intrusion did more to split the group than hold it together. Shann argues that 'centrifugal forces in the Bussell family' were held in check only by growing tension between the settlers and the Aboriginal people on the Vasse. In 1841 this culminated in a murder by the Aborigines and a massacre (or massacres) by the Europeans in which the Bussell men were directly involved, after which 'the Vasse had rest from the natives'.[49] After this the joint estate was gradually divided, firstly to provide for the married sisters, then in 1844 in a division of land and stock and machinery between brothers and mother and unmarried sister.[50]

The division sharply reduced John and Charlotte's resources and income. Charlotte was by this time keeping the accounts, a task previously done by her sisters-in-law. She noted that 'in order to preserve for his wife and children [now five in number] a comfortable dwelling', John had given up his share in all the family equipment—mill, carts, ploughs, harrows, threshing machine and working animals. He further reduced his portion by insisting that both his mother and his unmarried sister Fanny should have a home and an income for life; 'thus Fanny will be spared the feeling of being dependent on her brothers'. John 'still is, as he ever has been through life', observed Charlotte, 'most generous and disinterested in things financial'.[51] She concluded that John would need to be 'busy with his hands', and she 'must be equally active in the endeavour to raise funds by every means in my power that may be lawful', in the first instance by 'storekeeping'—trading farm produce and imported goods with the smaller settlers and ship's crews that visited the bay, notably American whalers.[52]

Women's labour had always been an important part of the family enterprise, both the domestic tasks that fed, clothed, housed and kept the workers clean, and the tasks like dairying and poultry keeping that contributed more directly to the family income. By 1840 sales of butter, cheese, poultry and fruit and vegetables—all the work of women—were the second most valuable item in the accounts, second only to the sale of stock.[53] This was a fact not directly recognised in the debates about the division of 'the firm of Bussell Bros.';[54] provision was made for the sisters more as charity—to save them from 'unbecoming' toil[55]—than in recognition of their real contribution. But colonial circumstances continued to encourage a very active role for women in enterprises that belonged formally and legally to their husbands.

Children also worked much harder than did their cousins in England. Charlotte's elder daughter by her first marriage was a constant help in caring for the baby girls born in western Australia.[56] In 1848, when his stepchildren had returned to school in England and the family was completely without servants, John Bussell enlisted the aid of his 9-year-old daughter to milk all the cows, while Charlotte looked after the dairy (and a toddler). During the day two daughters went with John to tend the family's sheep; 'no hardship', reported Charlotte, as the sheep 'coil under a shady tree and there John sits and reads to his bairns. They take out their books with them and learn their lessons too'.[57]

Even allowing for her resolve not to write sad letters, Charlotte's correspondence in these years suggests a contented woman, deeply involved in the family enterprise. In the early 1850s the coming of convict labour made it possible for husband and wife to take a less strenuous, more managerial role. Charlotte's response was to push for an expansion of the business: 'Had we the funds now to employ 3 or 4 men and to purchase 2 or 3 hundred sheep, our returns would be 5 or 6 hundred a year, and with that we should be enabled to make *ten times* as much'. In an assertion of colonial virtue she tells her English correspondent: 'A farm life still interests me exceedingly and very much do I continue to enjoy the life I lead here, and so would *you* dearest'.[58]

By the mid-1850s management of the farm was clearly a joint exercise. Charlotte even suggests that she is more immediately in touch with events than John. She complains that she can never finish a letter because

> John hates to see me at my desk . . . and always makes a point of talking to me more at such times than at any other asking me all sorts of puzzling questions with regard to dates what day this, that and the other were done—when the potatoes were planted—when a bullock was last killed, etc. etc. [This] puts an end to this mental chat I am having with you . . . unless I go down into my own room, which he cannot bear me to do.[59]

Here is true indispensability, at once as companion and as business partner.

In 1858, when she was fifty years old, Charlotte travelled alone around the continent to visit her brother's sheep station in outback New South Wales. She wrote John a letter full of the practical details of sheep management—how to pen the lambing ewes, how to choose the best breeding stock, the right way to wash the wool—all presented as urgent suggestions for improvement at Cattle Chosen.[60]

> In April next you must put the rams into the fold and not before, and you must allow two rams for every hundred ewes. If you have a less number a great many of the ewes will not lamb. Some consider three rams necessary for every hundred, so, dearest, you must increase your number forthwith, if you have not already done so.

She was equally firm in instructing him to fetch her from King George's Sound, where her steamer would set her down; do 'not let the difficulty of the undertaking annoy you. As to the funds, something will turn up . . .'. In the event, it didn't, and neither did John. But Charlotte found other relatives to support her.

In the years that followed John and Charlotte were increasingly apart. John travelled quite often to Perth as part of his duties as a magistrate, and later as a member of the Legislative Council. Charlotte took advantage of better roads and shipping to visit daughters and friends around the colony. In 1864 and 1865 John lived and worked in Perth as the master in charge of the seven boys enrolled in Western Australia's only secondary school, Bishop's School. The bishop cited as his qualifications for the job his classical scholarship—and indeed he continued to compose 'very fair' Latin verses in the wilds[61] and his 'aptitude for drawing out the mental powers of young people, and giving them a taste for reading'. The proof of this was his own family, all 'great readers of Shakespeare', thanks to John's 'culture and kindliness'.[62]

But separation did not make the couple more distant. John Bussell the philosopher continued as John Bussell the farmer to worry his wife with questions about the running of the estate. After a dozen letters from her husband, Charlotte declared that she wanted no more 'questions about Bulls, Horses, Pigs, Sheep and Sheep Ointment, Branding etc. etc.', and demanded that 'all topics on farming and cattle and sheep, oxen and servants be dropped in our correspondence forthwith'. Rather she wanted 'a little account of your every day goings on . . . which is your favourite among the boys, if they . . . seem to benefit by your mode of teaching . . . I require a change in the current of my thoughts once a week at least, by the perusal of your *delightful letters*'.[63]

A week later she wrote more plainly; she felt that John's instructions did not recognise her authority on the estate. She had not delivered John's message to the men

> because I think their behaviour is caused more by my Argus eyes than interest for you. They know nothing escapes my observation . . . and they know if they do not work well and diligently they would have to leave forthwith, for I cannot keep any drones about me in these hard days.[64]

John acquiesced, with his usual affectionate irony. The next month he wrote that he had been trying to find her 'a long piece of gossip this week, as I have been to parties and such things as make news for female ears'. He concluded with real feeling:[65]

> A short month and I shall be with you, it is morning before breakfast, the approach of the time of once more embracing you, dearest, freshens up all the feelings which length of time has rendered less intolerable. Adieu with love all round and believe me, your loving J.G.B.

Charlotte expresses no sense of personal loss at his absence, and welcomes his presence mainly because it allows her 'to do many little things for his comfort'—to cut his hair, get him some new collars, cover his hat . . .[66] For her love was still a question of making herself useful, though she no longer needed to be indispensable.

Charlotte Bussell

In September 1875 John Bussell fell suddenly ill with pneumonia at Cattle Chosen. Charlotte hurried back from Perth, but he died before she arrived. A sister-in-law commented a little tartly: 'Poor Charlotte . . . had not even the mournful satisfaction of tending him to the last. How often it must recur to her that on others devolved the wife's tender watching and care'.[67]

Early in 1875, Charlotte had inherited a modest fortune from her brothers' estates, and she and her husband were preparing to visit England at the time of his death. It was a journey they had often spoken of, but never been able to afford. Three months after John's funeral she and an unmarried daughter embarked for Europe. They toured England, beginning with John's old home in Winchester and his college at Oxford, where they 'wandered about in the gardens . . . thinking of him whom we never forget'.[68] In 1878 they settled in Paris, and Charlotte lived there until she died in 1899.

Charlotte wrote long affectionate letters to her family, and entertained a succession of granddaughters in Paris. But she had no desire to return to Western Australia. Once she compared herself to old Mrs Bussell:[69]

> Poor Grandmama! it was a mistake her leaving England—her pretty home at Winchester, her life long friends . . . to live as she thought a happy contented life in W. A. surrounded by her sons and daughters. The reality proved so different to what she had expected, for they were all so much occupied to devote much time to her . . . I often think of Grandmama's disappointment . . . and feel it would be the *same with me*.

John and Charlotte brought complementary expectations to Cattle Chosen. Both subscribed to the evangelical ideal which supposed man to be the supporting oak, woman the clinging vine,[70] though his idea of manhood was more heroically active than a standing tree, and her idea of womanhood more useful than an ornamental creeper. He had hoped for a wife who would love him for his manly authority, she a husband who would love her for her womanly competence. The unfamiliar colonial soil nourished some aspects of their sense of self and left others to wither. If her competence outgrew his heroism, both continued to be sustained by deep-rooted affection. And though John was the first to embrace the wilderness, it was Charlotte who was transformed by the colonial environment, losing in the end her need to be needed.

Lives in exile: Elizabeth and John Macarthur

Hazel King

Elizabeth Veale was born in the village of Bridgerule, in Devonshire, in August 1766. Her father, Richard Veale, was a yeoman farmer who owned 'Lodgeworthy', a farm of about 94 acres. At Lodgeworthy, mists from the sea 5 miles away, frequent showers and the melted snows of winter keep the fields green and damp. The house and farm buildings are built around a farmyard and to the back of them lies a garden, bright with flowers in the springtime, when May trees and flowers also bloom on the high banks of the lanes round about. In such surroundings Elizabeth spent her childhood, but her life contained a very different destiny. As a result of her marriage to John Macarthur in 1788, she spent most of her life in a vast, dry, sunburnt country on the other side of the world, divided from her beloved mother, and for long periods divided also from her children and even from the husband for whose sake she cheerfully endured this exile.

Before Elizabeth turned six her father died, aged thirty-two. Unable to continue living at Lodgeworthy, Elizabeth and her mother lived together in Bridgerule until her mother remarried in 1778. At about this time Elizabeth went to live with her grandfather, John Hatherley.[1] Although her only sister had died at the age of two, Elizabeth's was not a lonely childhood. She spent a great deal of time, as she was growing up, with the family of the Reverend John Kingdon, the vicar of Bridgerule. In later years his elder daughter Bridget wrote of herself and Elizabeth as having been brought up together as intimate friends. Probably Elizabeth was educated with the Kingdon children, partly by a governess and partly by the Reverend John Kingdon himself, who was a former Fellow of Exeter College, Oxford.[2] Elizabeth certainly showed herself later, through her letters, her love of books and reading, and the value she placed on education for her own children, to have been well educated. She is unlikely to have been so had she merely attended the village school. The Kingdon family certainly played a very significant part in her life when young and she corresponded with them and remembered them with great affection till she was an old woman.

It was through the Kingdons that Elizabeth met young John Macarthur. He was the son of Alexander Macarthur, a linen draper of Plymouth Dock. The exact date of John's birth is not known but it is recorded that he was baptised in Stoke Damerel Church, Devonport, in September 1767. His age at baptism is not known. Little is known of his youth except that his mother died in 1777 when he was about ten years old. He was educated at a private school in the country.

When he was about fifteen, in 1782, John entered the army as an ensign in a corps of foot, which had been raised for service against the rebellious colonies in North America. He never served in America, however, for less than a year after he had been commissioned, England recognised the independence of her former colonies, the British army was substantially reduced and John was put on half-pay. The half-pay of an ensign would hardly have been enough for him to live on and probably his father gave him an allowance. In later years his antagonists in New South Wales alleged that he had become a stay-maker's apprentice, but I have found no evidence to support this. It is not clear why he went to live near Bridgerule, where he is said to have lived in a farmhouse and to have thought of studying law.[3] It was probably at this period of his life that he acquired some knowledge of farming.

It was certainly during these years that he met Elizabeth Veale. In May 1788 he and she stood as godparents at the baptism of Elizabeth Dennis Kingdon, younger daughter of the Reverend John Kingdon. Just two weeks before this, John had once more gone on full army pay as an ensign, this time in the 68th Regiment of Foot. Six months later, in October 1788, he and Elizabeth were married. The ceremony was performed by licence by the Reverend John Kingdon at Bridgerule. That it was performed by licence meant that it had been arranged in some haste. Five months later their eldest son, Edward, was born at Bath when the young couple were on their way to London.

That a child was born so soon after marriage would generally have been considered shameful among the middle classes during the nineteenth century. But in the eighteenth century it may not have been considered so shocking. Until 1753 a verbal contract of marriage was deemed a valid marriage for many purposes and a betrothal was regarded as being virtually as binding as a marriage.[4] Probably John and Elizabeth were already betrothed when they stood as co-godparents the previous May; if they had plighted their troth, Elizabeth may well have regarded herself as already being John's wife before the actual marriage ceremony was performed. It is possible, also, that John was absent from Bridgerule for a time in connection with his military appointment and this may have delayed the performance of the ceremony. Or perhaps it was simply that they were a young couple so deeply in love that momentarily they forgot all else.

Some weeks before his wedding, John had obtained permission to delay for two months joining his regiment, which was stationed in Gibraltar. He was in fact never to join the 68th, for in 1789, with the rank of lieutenant, he exchanged into the NSW Corps which was being formed under the command of Major Grose. His pay as lieutenant was 3s 6d a day, which was not very much, even in those days, on which to keep a wife and child. Elizabeth had no marriage settlement to boost the family's income. Neither of them can be said to have married for money. Few of her friends, wrote Elizabeth at a later date, thought that they had been prudent to marry: 'I was considered indolent and inactive: Mr. Macarthur too proud and haughty for our humble fortune and expectations'. He was ambitious, self-confident, and believed he could do better in New South Wales than he could by doing garrison duty at Gibraltar.

Elizabeth wrote optimistically to her mother in October 1789 from Chatham, where the NSW Corps was mustered. She emphasised the economic advantages of Macarthur's decision rather than the impending separation. They had every reasonable expectation, she wrote, of reaping the most material advantages in the new land:

> You will be surprised that even I, who appear timid and irresolute, should be a warm advocate of this scheme. So it is, and . . . I shall be greatly disappointed if anything happens to impede it. I foresee how terrific and gloomy this will appear to you. To me at first it had the same appearance . . . I have not now . . . one scruple of regret, but what relates to

you ... If we must be distant from each other, it is much the same whether I am two hundred or far more than as many thousand miles apart from you. The same Providence will watch over and protect us there as here.

In the country to which she was going, she continued, nature had been lavish in her bounties, flowers abounded luxuriantly, and, with

Elizabeth Macarthur, portrait by an unknown artist

cultivation, fruits would do the same. According to the latest accounts from the colony, she said, wheat had been sown and flourished in an incredible manner, building was making rapid progress, and by the time they arrived, everything would be made comfortable for them.[5] The first accounts of the settlement in Sydney Cove had arrived some months before, and had not been unfavourable. But very little was known, as yet, about the vast, unexplored land at the other side of the world.

On Friday 13 November the Macarthurs boarded the transport *Neptune* near Gravesend. After beating up and down the Channel in unfavourable weather for two weeks, they dropped anchor in Plymouth. That afternoon Macarthur went ashore with Surgeon Harris and, as Elizabeth later discovered to her great consternation, he fought a duel with Gilbert, the Master of the ship, with whom he had fallen out on the day after they had gone on board. Neither man was wounded, but it was an early indication of John's propensity to fall into dispute, which was to have such a disruptive impact on the later course of their married life. Two days later Elizabeth, baby Edward and his nurse, left for Bridgerule to pay a last brief visit to her mother and friends. She was never to see them again. John would return twice to England, and several of their children would make the journey Home to be educated and even to live and die there, but for Elizabeth the exile was permanent and unrelieved.

When she returned to Plymouth, she found that there was a state of minor warfare between Gilbert and the military. They sailed ten days later and turned back to Portsmouth to rendezvous with the transports *Scarborough* and *Surprise*, which completed the Second Fleet. At Portsmouth it was with relief that they learnt that the objectionable Mr Gilbert was to be removed from his command and replaced by Mr Traill. Elizabeth wrote in her journal:

> Heartily glad I was when he made his exit and we congratulated ourselves with the thought that such another *troublesome* man could not be found, and consequently our change must be for the better. Experience, however, soon taught us a very disagreeable truth, Mr. Traill's character was of a much blacker dye.[6]

Later she described him as 'a perfect sea-monster'.

The unfortunate convicts on the *Neptune*, about 500 of them, were shown an even blacker side of Traill's character than was Elizabeth Macarthur. They were starved, brutally treated, heavily ironed, kept below and seldom allowed access to sun and air on deck. One hundred and fifty-seven of them died on the voyage; of the 269 who landed sick, many died soon afterwards. All were emaciated and so weak they were scarcely able to walk. In the other ships the condition of the convicts was not much better. The mortality rate in the Second Fleet was the highest in the whole shameful history of transportation to Australia.

Although Elizabeth's sufferings on the voyage were not like those of the convicts, they were bad enough. Owing to bad weather they did not leave England until 17 January 1790. In the Bay of Biscay they encountered tempestuous weather and for the first time her courage failed her: 'I began to be a coward', she wrote. 'I could not be persuaded that the ship could possibly long resist the violence of the sea which ran mountains high.' Then when the seas abated her infant son became very ill and her maidservant caught the fever which was raging among the convicts. Elizabeth dreaded lest they should all catch it.

Their accommodation was very cramped. The cabin originally allotted to the Macarthurs had been divided by a light partition and half the cabin was occupied by women convicts. As they approached the Equator the heat and stench in the cabin became almost unbearable. The rations were cut down and they were allowed only 5 quarts of water a day for all purposes. And Elizabeth had to listen to what she called the 'dreadful imprecations and shocking discourses' of the convicts who surrounded the cabin.[7] It was a far cry from the Vicarage, the quiet green fields and flowery lanes of Devonshire.

Things were much better, however, after John managed to arrange, while they were still at sea, that his family be transferred to the *Scarborough*. Here they shared a small cabin with another lieutenant of the Corps and his wife. For Elizabeth it was heaven after the horrors of the *Neptune*, and Mr Marshall, the ship's Master, whom she described as a 'plain honest man', made them as comfortable as he could. They reached the Cape of Good Hope, where they spent sixteen blissful days, about three months after leaving England.

The latter part of the voyage brought fresh trials, for John became very ill with rheumatic fever; 'every sense was lost and every faculty but life destroyed', wrote Elizabeth. At the same time, baby Edward became so ill that she did not expect him to survive. She herself was pregnant and prematurely gave birth to a daughter, who died within an hour.[8] At last, in June 1790, six months after they had embarked, they arrived in Port Jackson.

Elizabeth's first letters from Sydney have not survived, but if she had really expected comfortable buildings and flourishing corn, she must have been sorely disappointed. For they found wattle-and-daub huts, a few ramshackle houses, and the little community emaciated and weak from having been for months on short rations. The sick and dying convicts, who were slung ashore when the Second Fleet arrived, added to the plethora of human misery in the tiny settlement.

By March 1791, however, when Elizabeth again wrote to her mother and Bridget Kingdon, she was in an optimistic mood. John had been seriously ill again after their arrival but by the end of the year had recovered and in January 1791 they had been moved into a more convenient house. It was commodious enough to accommodate a piano, the property of Surgeon Worgan, which he was teaching her to play. Edward, although small and backward, had survived the voyage and delighted his parents by beginning to prattle. Although she found the heat of her first Australian summer almost unbearable, she took an interest in her strange surroundings. She tried to make a garden, but in March when she wrote it was all burnt up; she believed that the soil was quite unsuited for growing European plants. But she delighted in the native plants and flowers and the landscape which she found 'charmingly turned and diversified by agreeable valleys and gently rising hills'.

Her interest in her surroundings was in part a compensation for a 'certain vacancy' in her time in this very male world. She lamented the lack of opportunity for conversation: 'having no female friend to unbend my mind to, nor a single woman with whom I could converse with any satisfaction to myself, the clergyman's wife being a person in whose society I could reap neither profit nor pleasure'. Isolated by both her social position and her femininity, she began to study botany under the instruction of Mr Dawes, an officer of the Marines, and felt that she had made some progress: 'I have arrived so far as to be able to class and order all common plants. I have found great pleasure in my study: every walk furnished me with subjects to put in practice that theory I had before gained by reading.' She had also tried to learn astronomy, and had put Mr Dawes to much trouble in making orreries for her and explaining 'the general principles of the heavenly bodies'. But she found it too difficult, and confessed to Bridget, 'I had mistaken my abilities, and blush at my error'. In a society in which there were very few women who were not convicts, lonely young officers naturally sought the company of the attractive Elizabeth. Even Governor Phillip daily sent her fruit or 'some little thing or other'.[9] But Elizabeth's own hunger for the companionship of other women was rarely assuaged in these early years.

In the following year, the Macarthurs' third child, Elizabeth, was born. After that the babies came in rapid succession: John, named after his father, Mary, born in 1795, then James, named after his uncle in Plymouth. To his mother's deep grief, he lived for less than twelve months.

Meanwhile, Macarthur had been given his first land grant, 10 acres at Parramatta which he named Elizabeth Farm in honour of his wife. Here they built their own home, a brick cottage which, with later additions, was to remain Elizabeth's much-loved home for the rest of her life. John's hopes of doing well for himself in New South Wales were being fulfilled. He was appointed Paymaster of the NSW Corps, was promoted to the rank of captain, and for several years, until he resigned after a quarrel with Governor Hunter, he also held the civil post of inspector of public works. Elizabeth was more than

A pencil sketch by Charles Rodius of a cottage at Camden, in 1834

contented with her lot. In her isolation she was very dependent on her husband for companionship, but seemed to feel that John provided this in full measure. She wrote to Bridget Kingdon:

> I can truly say no two people on earth can be happier than we are. In Mr. Macarthur's society I experience the tenderest affections of a husband, who is instructive and cheerful as a companion. He is an indulgent Father, beloved as a Master, and universally respected for the integrity of his character.

Not everyone, of course, would have agreed with this assessment. Macarthur's uncertain temper and quarrelsome disposition were already earning him enemies in the colony, and would eventually involve him in disputes which entailed his long absences in England. Elizabeth did not suffer directly from his temper, but she would suffer its consequences in long years of separation.

Elizabeth busied herself making a garden and supervising her dairy. Major Grose had given them 'a very fine cow in calf; . . . to a family in this country in its present situation it is a gift beyond any value that can be placed upon it'.[10] There were as yet very few domestic animals in the colony and to a mother with young children a cow and her milk was indeed a gift of great price.

The first break in the family circle came in 1797 when Edward, at the age of eight, sailed for England where he was to go to school. It was heartbreaking for Elizabeth to part with the little boy who had been so delicate and who, but for her care, would probably have died in infancy. She also had fears about the voyage the little boy had to undergo. England was at war with France, and to the usual perils and discomforts of the long voyage was added the risk of enemy action. She was comforted the following year, however, by the arrival of another baby to care for when James the second, named after his uncle and dead brother, was born. In 1800 came William, the youngest son. Elizabeth had borne eight children in eleven years, six of whom had survived infancy.

Family life was again disrupted in 1801 when Macarthur, always proud, touchy and hot-tempered, and an arch-troublemaker according to Acting Governor King, fought a duel with Colonel Paterson, his commanding officer. Paterson was seriously wounded and King promptly put Macarthur under arrest. Being convinced that there would be no tranquillity in the colony while the 'perturbator', as he called him, remained in it, King ordered him to go to England under open arrest so that the home authorities could deal with the matter.

He told the Under Secretary of State that Macarthur had 'come here in 1790 more than £500 in debt, and is now worth at least £20,000'.

Although King may have exaggerated the extent of Macarthur's wealth, he had undoubtedly prospered. He had about 3500 acres of land acquired in part by grant and in part by purchase. It was worked by convict labour. He had some 4000 sheep and had begun his experiments in breeding for fine wool. As ordered, he sailed for England in November 1801. He took two more children with him to be educated in England—his eldest daughter, Elizabeth, aged nine, and young John, aged seven. Separation from their children was perhaps the harshest aspect of the colonial experience for parents, but, particularly for sons, education was a priority. Elizabeth never saw her son John again, for he made his career in England and died in his early thirties without having returned to Australia. In the meantime she was left with three small children under the age of six to bring up with little assistance. For the next four years she would combine this responsibility with that of managing her husband's properties and business affairs. Unfortunately her letters to her husband during this period and during his second, longer absence from the colony have not survived.

The independent management of the estate represented a burden rather than a privilege to Elizabeth. Communications with England were few, uncertain and slow and as week after week passed without a word, she was a prey to anxiety. In 1804 she wrote to Captain Piper:

> the management of our concerns gets troublesome to me in the extreme and I am perpetually annoyed by some vexation or other . . . God grant me Health and Patience, for indeed my good friend, I have need of *both* to keep my mind in tolerable frame.[11]

Despite her anxieties she faced her responsibilities courageously, and under her management the Macarthurs' sheep and other livestock increased in numbers. Early in 1805 their sheep were estimated to number over 4000, nearly a quarter of all the sheep in the colony. Labour was always a problem, which became more acute as the number of convicts assigned to them diminished.

Elizabeth faced danger when in 1804 the Irish convicts rose and she and her children had to flee from Parramatta. She was at the Reverend Samuel Marsden's home one evening when news was brought that 'the Croppies' had risen and were at the Macarthurs'

Seven Hills and Pennant Hills farms. They were approaching Parramatta. Mrs Marsden and Elizabeth, with their children, hastened to the barracks where they were advised to go to Sydney by boat. They arrived there at 3 a.m. to find the town in arms. The Governor, officers and soldiers had already left for Parramatta and a number of armed marines and sailors from HMS *Calcutta* were patrolling the streets. 'Our little *frightened, sleepy* tribe were escorted [to their accommodation] and civilities were poured in upon us from every quarter', wrote Elizabeth. In Parramatta the rising was ruthlessly suppressed, and within a few days Elizabeth and Mrs Marsden were told by the Governor that they might safely return to their homes. It was later learnt that the rebels had planned to set fire to Elizabeth's home as they knew of her lonely situation and thought that the soldiers would immediately go in strength to her aid. The defence of the barracks would thus be weakened and the rebels might more easily capture them.[12]

Meanwhile it had taken over a year for John and the children to reach England and it was more than a year after their arrival in London that a decision on Macarthur's case was reached. He was not brought before a court martial because the authorities decided that it was impossible to hold one in England with any hope of arriving at a just decision. Only one of the people involved in the duel was available to give evidence, and none of the witnesses. Macarthur was therefore relieved of his arrest and ordered to return to New South Wales to rejoin his regiment. He did not do so, however, for he succeeded in obtaining permission to sell his commission and to retire from the army.

While he had been awaiting a decision on his case, he had shown samples of wool grown by his sheep to wool textile manufacturers, who had been favourably impressed by its quality. He had approached the Under Secretary in charge of the affairs of New South Wales and other officials, and proposed plans to increase the quantity of wool produced. He had given evidence to the same effect before a Committee of the Privy Council for Trade and Foreign Plantations. He had been able to show that, since he had begun crossing Spanish Merino rams with ewes of mixed breed, their numbers had increased and the weight and quality of their fleeces had improved. He argued that New South Wales was particularly suited in regard to climate and pasturage to the production of fine wool. He asserted that, with proper management, the colony could ultimately supply all Britain's wool needs and she would no longer be dependent upon a foreign source. Spain had hitherto been the principal source of supply for the British wool textile industry and in time of war the continuity of the supply could be threatened. Macarthur further argued that the development of wool production could provide a field for the employment of convicts. If wool growers maintained those convicts who were assigned to them, the government would not be put to the expense of keeping them. Anything which lessened the cost of the expensive penal colony would undoubtedly appeal to the home government.

In September 1804, John Macarthur obtained an interview with Lord Camden, the Secretary of State for War and Colonies, the outcome of which was that he was promised a grant of land of 5000 acres in the first instance, with the promise of a further 5000 if the experiment proved successful. Camden also procured for him a Treasury Warrant authorising him to export stud merinos which he had bought from the Royal flock. Because the wool textile industry was of such importance to British trade, the export of sheep from England was at that time prohibited except by special authority.

So in October 1804 John and his precious sheep set out for home in his own ship, appropriately named the *Argo*, which he intended to use later in the whale fisheries. His nephew Hannibal Macarthur, two wool sorters, skilled mechanics and their families, a gardener and a number of servants travelled with him. His daughter Elizabeth was thought to be too delicate to be left at school in England and, accompanied by her governess, Miss Penelope Lucas, she too travelled on the ship. Miss Lucas, who became her mother's trusted friend, remained with the family for the rest of her life. The two boys, Edward and John, remained in England to continue their education.

The *Argo* arrived in Sydney in June 1805 and Elizabeth had a few happy years with her husband and four of her children, grieving only for the two sons who were so far away from her. John, meanwhile, had some difficulty in obtaining his grant of 5000 acres in the area which he had picked out before he left Australia in 1801. This was in the Cowpastures, where the government herd of wild cattle roamed and multiplied. Governor King was reluctant to grant him land there and did so only because instructed by Lord Camden to comply with John's wishes in regard to locality. Even then he made the grant provisional only. King and Macarthur had patched up their differences, at least on the surface, and when the time came for the Kings to depart, 'we parted with regret' as Elizabeth put it. Her regrets would have been even deeper had she foreseen what would happen during the reign of King's successor, Governor Bligh.

The extent to which John Macarthur may have engineered the so called 'Rum Rebellion', when Bligh was deposed and power seized by Major Johnston and the NSW Corps, is a controversial subject. The home government certainly regarded him as being deeply involved and when Johnston was himself deposed and sent home to face court martial, Macarthur felt it prudent to go also to put his case before the authorities. He left Sydney in March 1809 taking with him his two younger sons, James and William, like their brothers to be educated in England. He left just in time, for a few months later Governor Macquarie, who had succeeded Bligh, was ordered to have him arrested and brought to trial before the Criminal Court of the colony. As a civilian he could not be court-martialled. Neither he nor Elizabeth dreamt that they would be separated for over eight years.

During the previous year, at the age of forty-two, Elizabeth had given birth to her ninth child, Emmeline, the baby and darling of the whole family. Once again Elizabeth was left with John's properties and business affairs to manage, which were more extensive and varied than previously. Her family responsibilities were also heavy. Elizabeth, her delicate eldest daughter, was so seriously ill when her father left that he did not expect her to live. Mary, their second daughter, was partly paralysed, and Emmeline was still an infant. 'Every day I feel ... an accumulated weight of responsibility and care', wrote Elizabeth a few months after her husband left.[13] At least she now had the friendship and support of Penelope Lucas, 'who shares all my cares', and who remained at Parramatta to care for and to chaperone the girls on the frequent occasions on which their mother had to be away from home to attend to John's affairs in Sydney or at Camden.

Elizabeth had no male member of the family to assist her for the first three and a half years of John's absence, for his nephew Hannibal was also away from Australia. After Hannibal's return, John increased his trading 'adventures', as he called them, and sent out large quantities of goods, the sale of which Hannibal was supposed to arrange. But John instructed him to follow his aunt's advice in all matters and she was expected to go over all the books and the accounts. So the responsibility remained with her. Elizabeth herself was happier looking after her husband's rural interests than his trading 'adventures'. She tried to dissuade him from undertaking them but was unable to do so.

Elizabeth Farm was by this time well established with gardens, orchard and a comfortable home, but the property on the Cowpastures, at the outer perimeter of explored land, was very different. Here, in 1810, Governor Macquarie and his wife, who were touring the region, met Elizabeth living in what Macquarie called a 'miserable hut', supervising the culling of sheep and cattle. Although she was the wife of a notorious rebel, whom he had been ordered to arrest, Elizabeth had by now some status in the colony on her own account, and Macquarie and his wife invariably treated her with great courtesy and kindness. They invited her to ride about the area with them that day and to dine with them at their camp in the evening before she returned to her 'miserable hut'. She also dined with them and was invited to attend functions at Government House when she was in Parramatta.

Elizabeth Farm, Parramatta, the home of John and Elizabeth Macarthur

On the property at the Cowpastures, her shepherds were all convicts but she had an emancipist overseer, Thomas Herbert, who drew up regular accounts of livestock. He was evidently a steady and reliable man for he remained in the Macarthurs' service from 1806 until his death in 1840. Constant effort was needed to manage the flocks, to cull and breed for fine wool, to protect them from marauders, to combat drought, fire and floods. The home flock of true merinos, kept for breeding purposes, was at Parramatta, the rest of the sheep scattered over the Cowpastures. Between 1813 and 1817 the Macarthur flocks averaged just over 4000 rising to over 5500 in 1814 and dropping to 3500 in 1816. In those early years there were no fenced grazing paddocks and every flock had a shepherd who drove it out to graze on the natural herbage during the day and drove it back to the folds each evening to be guarded at night. The lives of the shepherds, as well as those of the sheep, were at risk from Aborigines who were attempting to protect land and livelihood in the face of pastoral expansion. In 1816 Elizabeth wrote:

> I am much oppressed with care on account of our stock establishments at our distant farms, at the Cowpastures, having been disturbed by the incursions of the natives. The savages have burnt and destroyed the shepherds' habitations, and I daily hear of some fresh calamity ... Two years ago a faithful old servant ... was barbarous[ly] murdered by them and a poor defenceless woman also. Three of my people are now reported to be missing, but I trust they will be found unhurt.[14]

Shearing was done under primitive conditions, and the wool then stored in sheds until the only man in the colony capable of sorting it was available to do so. John complained that it often arrived in England in a dirty state, so it did not command the price that it should have done. Great efforts were then made to wash the sheep before they were shorn; to wash the wool afterwards would have been too costly. From time to time John complained that Elizabeth did not send him adequate stock returns and detailed accounts: 'Many important things escape your memory at the moment of writing. Do adopt the practice of making short memos when anything occurs worth repeating ... and include the Horses in your next Returns'. Although he scolded her from time to time for not keeping him fully informed, he also praised her:

> I am perfectly aware, my beloved wife, of the difficulties you have to contend with, and fully convinced that not one woman in a thousand, (no one I know) would have the resolution and perseverance to contend

with them all, much more to surmount them in the manner that you have so happily done. That I am grateful and delighted with your conduct I think is needless for me to say.[15]

Added to Elizabeth's cares and anxieties over her husband's affairs was worry about her son Edward, who had joined the British army as an officer when he returned to England in 1808 after he had paid a short visit to his parents. He had seen much active service in Spain and elsewhere during the Napoleonic Wars and had constantly been in danger. He had come through unscathed.

Meanwhile, with the help of influential friends, John Macarthur had at last succeeded in getting the Secretary of State to sanction his return to New South Wales. He was longing to be with Elizabeth who would, he wrote, cheer him with her approving smiles and reward him with the endearments to which he had for so long been a stranger. He sailed on the *Lord Eldon* in March 1817, arriving in Port Jackson the following September. His sons James and William returned with him, overjoyed to be reunited with the mother from whom they had been separated since they were young boys. The two elder sons remained in Europe to pursue their careers, Edward in the army and John as a barrister.

Her husband had already instructed Elizabeth to have 8 or 10 acres prepared at Parramatta and a few at the Cowpastures for the seeds and plants he was bringing with him. When the war had ended he, James and William had travelled in France and Switzerland noting methods of irrigation, of olive, vine and silk culture, which he intended to try in New South Wales. He brought with him on the *Lord Eldon*, in a greenhouse built on deck, cuttings and seeds collected from Europe and at Rio de Janiero when the ship called there. The hold was full of the latest agricultural implements.

Elizabeth was deeply thankful when they arrived. Two months after their return she wrote:

> I am yet scarcely sensible of the extent of my happiness, and indeed I can hardly persuade myself that so many of the dear members of our family are united again under the same roof. Mr Macarthur is occasionally afflicted with Gout, otherwise I perceive little change in him during this length of time. James and William from little Boys when they left me, returned fine young men.

She had no regrets but rather relief at relinquishing the management of her husband's affairs and resuming once more what she regarded as the proper role of a wife and mother. But no doubt John, who had so high an opinion of her capabilities, kept her informed and discussed his affairs with her on many occasions. She had the joy of seeing her eldest son again when, early in 1824, he obtained leave from his regiment and came home on a visit. 'The return of our beloved son Edward after an absence of sixteen years, was an event so joyful to us that I hardly yet think of it calmly', she wrote two months after his arrival.[16] He was now thirty-six years old, a captain, with years of hard military service behind him. He stayed ten months, which was all too short a time for his mother. She never saw him again, for he did not return to Australia until after her death.

John's return did not bring the tranquillity which Elizabeth had hoped for. He fell out with succeeding governors, with officials and with other colonists and was several times involved in lawsuits. His sufferings from gout increased and his health, both mental and physical, fluctuated. He would be sunk in deep depression for months at a time succeeded by periods of frantic activity. During one of the latter he began altering and renovating Elizabeth Farm. The work proceeded by fits and starts, plans made and scrapped, work demolished and started again. Elizabeth was excluded from her home for many months in 1826 and 1827 while the alterations were in progress. During this time she stayed in Woolloomooloo with her daughter Mary, who had married James Bowman, the Principal Surgeon. Perhaps these separations marked the commencement of the divisions and suspicion which were to cast a shadow over the last years of her married life.

Macarthur's alternating periods of depression and activity continued until 1831, when a great sorrow overtook him and Elizabeth. They received news of the death in London of their son John. Elizabeth grieved deeply for the son whom she had not seen since he was seven years old. To his father, who had watched over him in England as he was growing up, cared for and guided him, who took great pride in his intellectual ability and expected that he would have a brilliant career, the blow was overwhelming.

Although at first he bore his sorrow bravely, John's mental instability soon became more marked. He became suspicious of all those around him. He thought his son-in-law, Dr Bowman, was trying to poison him. Accusing his daughters of robbing him and his wife of being unfaithful to him, he turned them out of the house.[17] Elizabeth again went to live with the Bowmans while her two unmarried daughters, chaperoned by the faithful Miss Lucas, lived

John Macarthur, c. 1817, portrait by an unknown artist

in the cottage at Elizabeth Farm (now called Hambledon Cottage), which Edward had occupied during his visit. Either James or William lived at Elizabeth Farm and supervised the care of their father while the other managed the properties. John was confined to the library and a small sleeping room. During 1832 he was declared insane and his sons were made his guardians. The following year his condition somewhat improved and he was taken, against his will, to Camden where, during his lucid periods, he occupied himself in supervising the building of the fine new house, Camden Park, which he had planned as the family home for them all. Early in 1834 his mental state again deteriorated; he died in April of the same year. 'The fountain of my Eyes, which I believed to have been nearly dryed, have opened anew', wrote Elizabeth to Edward.[18]

In his will, John left the wife who had carried so heavy a burden of responsibility, who had worked so hard and who had looked after his affairs so faithfully, an annuity to be paid her by her sons and the right to live at Elizabeth Farm. His unmarried daughters received annuities. To his three surviving sons he left all his properties, by now very extensive, and the stock.[19] Elizabeth does not appear to have resented this, nor to have wanted or expected anything else. It was a male-dominated world. During her husband's lifetime, she had had little money of her own. She had not even been able to make her mother comfortable by giving her a small allowance. But this was done, as she put it, 'through the generosity of Mr Macarthur'. After his death it was continued by her sons.

Another great sorrow came to Elizabeth in 1842 when her eldest daughter died. She had remained unmarried and had lived with her mother at Elizabeth Farm. 'Still I mourn, and tears flow when I think of her many virtues . . . to me she was the most devoted of daughters', wrote Elizabeth some months after her death.[20]

Life, since her marriage to the ambitious, tempestuous half-pay officer, had brought Elizabeth many troubles and deep grief, but her equable temperament, and her unshakeable belief that, as a Christian, she must bow to the will of God, brought her consolation. The years of hardship and separation transformed her from a woman in exile to a colonist in her own right. 'How grateful to the Almighty I ought to be for His many mercies!' she wrote to Edward on her eightieth birthday. She died in 1850 at the age of eighty-three.

Paradise lost: Sir John and Lady Jane Franklin

Penny Russell

Several years before her arrival in Van Diemen's Land, Lady Jane Franklin had sighed for 'simplicity & peace, & obscurity in some distant land, a land like Australia, where to breathe the very air is happiness, where sickness is turned into health, & existence, if existence could be conceived exempt from moral anxieties, . . . is in itself enjoyment'.[1] Before she had been there two years, as wife of the Lieutenant-Governor, Sir John Franklin, she was writing of her hopes to escape from 'this trying scene of incessant conflict and excitement though it would be necessary to leave the colony in order to secure entire exemption from it'.[2] Van Diemen's Land, it was all too clear, was a troubled paradise. It was inhabited by far too many serpents, the chief of whom, John Montagu, Colonial Secretary, was to be instrumental in having the Governor and his wife expelled from Eden. By the time the humiliating letter of recall arrived from the Secretary of State for the Colonies, the Franklins must have been glad to leave. The peace of obscurity had not been theirs. Every action they had taken had been under public scrutiny, and most had been loudly condemned. The uncomfortable notoriety intensified Jane's nervous illness and debility. Above all, the Franklins faced a particular 'moral anxiety' which was to become pivotal to the debate surrounding their recall: when did the support and assistance of a loving wife become intolerable interference with affairs of state?

Sir John Franklin, with his wife Lady Jane née Griffin, arrived in Van Diemen's Land in 1837 to take up his appointment as Lieutenant-Governor. He was fifty years old at the time, a naval

Jane Griffin, aged twenty-four, portrait by Amélie Romilly, 1816

captain renowned for his Arctic exploration. She was forty-five, a product of London's dilettante intellectual circles, and they had been married for eight years. Their life in Van Diemen's Land was to represent the most concentrated period of time they were ever to spend in each other's company, and must in many ways have been the most crucial period of their marriage. It was also the time when their relationship came under the most intense public scrutiny. They arrived in Van Diemen's Land with a strong shared vision for its future progress and development, seeing it as a free society in its infancy, which they would encourage and develop by promoting learning and culture. Jane worked energetically to assist Sir John in the achievement of these goals. From the outset she attracted criticism and condemnation, partly because the view of society the Franklins espoused was very unpopular among the gentry of Van Diemen's Land, and partly because her behaviour suggested that she thought she could assist Sir John as colleague and equal rather than as 'wife', as that term was narrowly understood in the colony. Ultimately her behaviour was to be represented by John Montagu as an unwarrantable interference in the affairs of government, and became a chief strand in his argument for their recall.

In Jane's own view, there was no limit to the proper devotion of a wife, even the wife of a governor. Marrying in her late thirties, Jane Griffin had had plenty of time in which to formulate her strong conviction that a wife should devote herself energetically and wholeheartedly to her husband's best interests. Her experiences had also led her to yearn for the opportunity to become totally committed to one man, without reservation and without deception. During her twenties she had been in the uncomfortable position of loving two men, unable to encourage either because of her confused sense of loyalty to both. One was a passionate, intelligent, Genevois physician, Adolphe Butini, the other was Dr Peter Mark Roget, who later compiled the Thesaurus. Butini courted her ardently, with his mother's enthusiastic assistance, during the Griffins' visit to Geneva in 1817. Jane resisted him, and he never actually declared his love, although it was common knowledge in Genevois society. But after her return to England in 1817 Jane seemed to have second thoughts. She was at this time attracted to Roget, and he appeared to return her feelings, but she felt unable to encourage him completely because of her sense of loyalty to Butini. Butini, or members of his family, occasionally appeared in England, but no clear denouement took place, and Jane yearned fruitlessly for the chance to explain her feelings directly with Butini himself. At last he abandoned hope, and yielded to the changing views of his family, who now felt that Jane's fortune was not a sufficient inducement. Jane was left to mourn his departure, and to lament that she had 'lost for ever in this world that being who has exerted the most fatal influence over my peace of mind, and he for whose sake I have lost him, has been pleading his suit to another. And what *now* remains to me?'.[3]

The torn loyalties and necessary deceptions of these relationships left Jane yearning for some stable object to whom she could be totally devoted. She consoled herself 'with the resolution that *whenever* I marry, *whoever* I marry, I will open my whole heart to him who will then possess supreme and exclusive dominion over it'. She dreamed of the stability of marriage. 'Shall I really make as good a wife as I intend to be?' she asked her diary, 'or is it one of my romantic fancies to think that the supremest bliss of a woman is to be found in her sanctified affection towards her husband?'[4]

By the time Butini and Roget married elsewhere, Jane seemed resigned to the impossibility of both relationships. Still, she persistently rejected other suitors. Her ideals of marriage were high, and as the daughter of a wealthy silk-weaver she had no need to regard her financial future with dread. Loneliness was the worst threat, and loneliness was infinitely preferable to the lack of independent choice. She retained her firm belief in the institution of marriage itself. When a friend told her that she hoped that her infant daughter would grow up to be a bluestocking so that she would never marry, Jane wrote, 'it was sad to think that she spoke sincerely'.[5]

Her single life was not devoted to the pursuit of matrimony. She was passionately committed to self-improvement, and after leaving boarding school was impelled to supplement the inadequate education she had received there with an intensive programme of private study. She did not live up to the high standards she set herself. At the bottom of an ambitious 'Plan for the employment of time and improvement of the mind, arranged according to the nature and relative importance of the studies necessary to be daily pursued', which she wrote at the age of nineteen, she added in later life the epitaph 'Alas! Alas!'.[6] But if she did not learn all the languages and philosophy she thought desirable, in her thirties she certainly possessed an enquiring, intelligent mind, broadened by extensive European travel, and she occupied a firm place in the intellectual circles of London. There was no expectation, in Jane or her family, that this preparation of her mind had any specific objective. As a spinster, she was engaged in a sort of dilettante intellectualism. As a married woman she was to dedicate her considerable talents and learning to furthering the career of her husband. Apparently even in her own view this was the only object to which a woman could avowedly devote her energy and ability.

In the early 1820s, in pursuit of intellectual company and amusement, Jane met and made friends with the young poet Eleanor Porden. Both women moved in the same circles and attended lectures at the fashionable Royal Institution. Eleanor was lively and irreverent; Jane perceived in her at times 'something very like vulgarity', but increasingly valued her friendship. That brief friendship ended with Eleanor's untimely death, but had a lasting impact on Jane's life, for it was through Eleanor that she met Captain John Franklin.

While Jane was enjoying the social and intellectual life of London, John Franklin had been making a name for himself in polar exploration. A lifelong lover of the sea and ships, he joined the Royal Navy early in life. As a midshipman he fought in several naval battles, but he also joined Matthew Flinders on his voyage of discovery to New Holland in 1801, and developed a particular interest in exploration. In 1818, as a lieutenant, he was chosen to accompany Captain David Buchan on a search for the North-West Passage. The expedition ended, to Franklin's bitter disappointment, in retreat, but meanwhile he had fallen in love with the Arctic. In the following year, he led a land expedition to Arctic America. It proved to be an experience of terrible suffering and deprivation, the laborious return trip dogged by near starvation and the spectre of death. The close encounter with death reinforced the impact of a censorious evangelical upbringing on a naturally earnest nature, and turned Franklin into a bleak and severe moralist. His return to London bewildered him. He had dealt better with the stark elements at their worst than he now dealt with the 'complexity and insincerity of civilized society'. Among the complexities was Eleanor Porden. Whether she represented this bewildering civilisation at its most charming, or offered him a life-raft to assist his survival in it, remains open to speculation. What is certain is that he fell in love with her, and, in 1823, married her.[7] Eleanor bore with good-natured teasing from Jane and Fanny Griffin, and in due course no doubt introduced her husband to the Griffin family.

John and Eleanor had some significant disputes over their respective faiths. Eleanor was not an evangelical, and was critical of John's censorious views. The issue was never resolved during her lifetime, but Kathleen Fitzpatrick, in a sensitive and perceptive discussion of this brief marriage, suggests that Eleanor's death may have had a

Captain John Franklin, naval commander and explorer, engraving by G. R. Lewis

lasting impact on John and his social and religious attitudes. Eleanor had promised that she would not hold him back from further Arctic exploration. She kept her promise, even though after a year of marriage she had an infant daughter and was dying of tuberculosis.

Though Franklin offered to forgo his command of a new expedition to Arctic America, Eleanor insisted that he should go.

Franklin sailed, and his first mail in America brought him the news of his wife's death. Fitzpatrick suggests that although John Franklin 'neither quite understood nor wholly approved' of Eleanor, his religious views may have been softened and his tolerance increased by 'the memory of the girl who did not believe in Sunday observance but who was willing to face death alone rather than break her word'. The experience also significantly affected his attitude to his second wife. He had learnt to respect Eleanor's intelligence and independence, and to appreciate the active and practical interest she had taken in his work. She had argued him out of his wish that she should cease her literary work on their marriage, writing, 'If you have liked what I really am, . . . I am willing to be yours. But you must not expect me to change my nature'. Her death reinforced the lessons of her life. Franklin's complete acceptance of Jane's independence, and his 'tender devotion' to her, can be seen as an act of reparation for 'his carelessness of his delicate first wife in the months before her death'.[8]

Franklin returned from his second Arctic American expedition in October 1827, bringing home a mass of geographical and scientific information. He was lionised by London society, and among the many happy to welcome him back were the Griffins. On his departure Jane and her sisters had all given him small gifts; the closeness of the acquaintance he had formed with the family was shown in the fact that he named a cape 'Point Griffin' after Jane's father. Soon after his return he brought presents of reindeer tongue and shoes for the ladies, in recognition of their kindness before his departure. That his relationship with Jane Griffin swiftly developed is clear, but Jane's diary for this period has apparently been suppressed. By July 1828 John was able to write to a friend that 'my affair in a certain quarter is finally fixed'.[9]

They were married in November 1828. John was 42 and Jane 37. Shortly before the marriage, Jane wrote John a letter indicating both her independent spirit, and her understanding of the real power relationships within marriage.

> Whenever I think I am imposed upon my spirit rises, and I struggle harder to resist than is perhaps consistent with the meek and resigned spirit which men endeavour to teach us is not only becoming but

obligatory, and which we poor women, endowed with acute sensibilities though with less energy and much less power than men, often find to be our surest and safest way to happiness.

As her 'beloved and most honoured husband' it would be John's duty to check this tendency 'when you think it improperly excited'. But having licensed him with this exercise of husbandly power, she undermined the mandate she had given him with some ironic humour.

> If you are a prudent man you will put this letter by and turn it to account on some future occasion when I am in a rebellious mood; and upon this consideration I think you ought to feel infinitely obliged to me for furnishing you with so valuable a document.[10]

There was irony in this, but there was also trust. Perhaps she already realised that John would not seek to check her independent thought and action by describing it as 'rebellious'.

Jane looked back on the first years of her marriage as a period of 'vanity, and trifling, and idleness'.[11] They were living in London, with Franklin's daughter Eleanor, waiting for Franklin to get another ship. Eventually, in the autumn of 1830, he was posted to the *Rainbow*, to be stationed in the Mediterranean. Jane endured some months of separation, and then resolved to join him there. In the period of his absence she wrote letters revealing her intense ambition for him and her devotion to his interests and himself, all of which seemed inextricably linked.

> My personal vanities and egoistic sensibilities have been absorbed in you ever since I married, and I feel no satisfaction in any sense of superiority, such as you attribute to me, but the greatest joy and purest delight in all that *you* possess over me.[12]

Her devotion was to him alone, rather than to a concept of family. She had acquired a stepdaughter, and did her best to love her and to bring her up to be of a good character, though she thought Eleanor had not 'the *beau ideal* of the female countenance or mind'. But Eleanor was not allowed to interfere with Jane's desire to join her husband in the Mediterranean. She left Eleanor behind in England, in part because of the threat of war, but also because 'I fear the child might sometimes be an obstacle to my being with you . . . I cannot resolve upon anything that is to separate me from you'.[13]

In the next few years Jane travelled in North Africa, Malta, Alexandria, Jerusalem. She was extending her knowledge of the world from Europe to areas far less frequented by English women, and there is every indication that she enjoyed the experience. Intense curiosity overrode discomfort and danger, and she found that her health improved when she was contending with difficulties rather than with idleness. The focus of all her travels, however, was Sir John—he was the nominal reason for her journeys, as well as the centre of them, though she spent more time without than with him.

In 1834 Franklin returned to England, and his wife followed after some months. She was anxious that he should find further employment, and he wrote to her of the efforts he had made in this direction, which included an audience with the King, and waiting on the First Lord of the Admiralty and the president of the Royal Society. 'You will fancy that your shy timid husband must have gathered some brass on his way home', he wrote to Jane, but added, 'I have done all but the truly official part principally because I knew you would have wished me to do so'.[14]

After Jane's return she suffered a nervous collapse from the cessation of danger and excitement. Homeless, out of work and in ill health, the Franklins wandered restlessly, visiting relatives and travelling to Ireland. In April 1836 Franklin was offered the lieutenant-governorship of Van Diemen's Land. He had earlier been invited to become the Lieutenant-Governor of Antigua, at half the salary, but although tempted himself by the offer, he declined to accept it until he had consulted his wife, who felt it was unworthy of him, and persuaded him to reject it.

These first years of marriage had set many of the patterns which were evident during their time in Van Diemen's Land. Jane's lack of physical health, accompanied by acute physical energy and zest for travel and adventure, were notable features of her life in the colony and were also the basis of many of the criticisms levelled at her. Her ill health led her to retire early from many government entertainments, creating the impression that she found them beneath her notice. Her travels to South Australia, New South Wales and New Zealand were inaccurately said to be a waste of public funds. Sir John's habit of consulting her in all the major decisions of his life, and his reliance on her judgement even when it went counter to his own, were also to have a negative impact in the colony. There was, however, a crucial difference in their relationship before and after the move to Van Diemen's Land. When they travelled, separately and together, around the Mediterranean, it was Sir John's interests which dictated their movements: he initiated, and Jane followed. Once she had followed him to Van Diemen's Land the nature of the relationship changed subtly. Now Sir John was tied to Hobart, often by dull administrative housekeeping, while Jane travelled more freely, and at her own will. The change might not have been a crucial one in terms of their personal relationship, but it certainly led to a totally different public interpretation being placed upon it. For the wife of a naval captain to follow her husband around might be deemed eccentric, but it was not unwomanly: it showed, indeed, a wifely devotion, and there were precedents for it in literature as in life. For the wife of a governor to neglect the social and domestic duties which in her case were quite rigidly codified, to leave the tasks of companion and hostess to others, went beyond eccentricity to culpability.

In Van Diemen's Land, the Franklins' relationship came under more critical public scrutiny than at any other period of their lives. From the beginning they found themselves at the centre of an entrenched hostility, which had its origins in the governorship of their predecessor, George Arthur. Arthur had surrounded himself with a group of colonial administrators, many of them related to him by marriage, who formed a power group devoted to their own distinct interests. The 'Arthur faction', led by the Colonial Secretary, John Montagu, consisted of experienced administrators, whose skills were essential to Franklin, though their interests were opposed to his. They formed a powerful clique in colonial society, exercising control not only in government but over the principal financial institution in the colony, the Derwent Bank. The arrival of a governor to replace Arthur offered a threat to their power, which they sought to overcome by using every means possible to defuse the Governor's power and retain most of it in their own hands. Moreover, their interests were directly opposed to Franklin's most cherished schemes. They represented the interests of the major landholders in the colony, which, they believed, could best be served by seeing it become, as Arthur had wished, the 'gaol of the empire'.[15]

Into this cosy world of vested interests erupted the Franklins, full of schemes to encourage an 'infant society' in the directions of culture and civilisation. They attempted to found a college for boys, they started a museum and formed the Tasmanian Society for

Jane as Lady Franklin, portrait by Thomas Bock

Natural History. They questioned the value and the cost of transportation and assignment to the colony, and in general represented a significant challenge to the stranglehold over the colony and its social development held by the landed gentry of the Arthur faction. Their efforts were regarded by the Arthur faction with contempt and ridicule, and met with constant obstruction.

Under these circumstances, Jane's wifely devotion took on a new significance. Throughout his period of governorship, Sir John needed her not merely as a companion but as an ally and support. He was by no means as incompetent as many of his colonial enemies liked to suggest. He demonstrated a firm grasp of the main problems confronting the colony. But his training had not been in administration, nor had he much experience in dealing with people and the petty power squabbles of colonial government. He knew his limitations and his inexperience; he lacked confidence and he worried.[16] To make matters worse, he had few friends that he could trust. His private secretary, Alexander Maconochie, soon proved more of a burden than an asset, mainly because of his single-minded devotion to the cause of penal reform, which occasionally interfered with his devotion to Sir John's interests, and which led to his dismissal in 1838. Sir John was forced into reliance on those experienced administrators who constituted his most frequent detractors, and increasingly he became aware that they were opposed to his chief interests and policies. In these circumstances, his only trustworthy confidant was his wife. She was very ready to discuss matters relating to colonial policy and transportation with him and other officials, and to offer her ideas, and she kept a keen eye out for political enemies. Particularly after Maconochie's dismissal, she assisted Sir John with his correspondence and other clerical work, and confided to her sister Mary as 'the *profoundest of secrets*' that an important despatch on transportation contained several ideas which she had suggested, while others were submitted to her 'for correction or alteration'.[17] This behaviour soon became one of the focuses of the Arthur faction's attack. From the outset her unconventionality had brought her under unfavourable notice, but as hostility to Franklin strengthened, and her importance to him as an ally was realised, she began to be represented as one of the worst aspects of his administration.

As Fitzpatrick points out, Jane was, for Sir John, the 'one individual in the colony on whose devotion and disinterestedness he could entirely rely'.[18] She supported and thus strengthened his aims for the colony, and with her intelligence and clear sight early warned him of the dangers which the Arthur faction represented to him. She was a formidable ally to her husband, a formidable enemy to his opponents, and they recognised this almost at once. As Sir John wrote, towards the end of his period of government,

> She cannot help being clever but that is what the Party cannot bear. They think they could have got on with a simple unsuspicious obstinate old fool like myself, but that her discernment has unveiled them, and it

is true she saw through them sooner than I did—but what then? Her desire has ever been to make the best of them, and if possible to keep them as friends in check, seeing how dangerous they would be as enemies.[19]

The Franklins made few concessions to their new and more public role in society. They seemed convinced that the nature of their devotion to each other had no bearing on their public position. John Franklin assumed that anything relating to his wife or his marriage belonged to his private life. Thus the extent to which Jane assisted him with his work could be of no possible interest to colonial society. When these activities were criticised as unwarrantable interference with affairs of state, Franklin tended to interpret the criticisms as unwarrantable interference with his private relationship. This view complemented Jane's own view of her proper duties as governor's wife. Towards the end of their time in Van Diemen's Land she wrote:

> With respect to my own conduct, I find myself guilty of being devoted to my husband, of trying to be of use to him, of yielding to his belief that I can be so, of exerting over him whatever influence I possess, not to magnify myself and gratify a love of power or distinction, but in furtherance, according to the best of my ability, of *his* interests, reputation and character.[20]

In fact, Jane was simply continuing the pattern of devotion to her husband's interests which had always characterised her. She wrote that the only gratification to her in her work was that she was thus 'enabled to be of use to Sir John'.

> You must not suppose that I think myself in a very extraordinary position and am a very wonderful person. I think quite the contrary. I suppose every woman whose husband is in public life helps him if she can and if he gives her the opportunity which he will not fail to do if he can trust in her ability and discretion, and as to the rest, no one knows half so well as myself the weakness of my faculties.[21]

In Van Diemen's Land, this devotion earned her violent hostility. Jane Franklin did not force herself into the public sphere. She was a part of it as soon as she set foot on colonial soil as the Governor's wife. It was her refusal to alter her interpretation of her marriage to meet the demands of her public role which brought shocked criticism down on her head. The stark light of publicity, fostered by a hostile colonial press, magnified wifely devotion into eccentric and inappropriate interest in the affairs of government and neglect of proper duties. Jane, who had always dreaded to be thought masculine or aggressive, and always denied that she was so, found herself caricatured as a 'man in petticoats', and it hurt.

Despite Jane's self-effacing estimate of her own powers, it can be argued that one of the reasons why the 'Party' could not bear Lady Franklin was that they feared that she wished to exert power in the colony as a woman, upsetting the structure of male dominance which had hitherto existed unchallenged. Convict society was essentially masculine and public: the majority of women in it were of convict origin themselves, and deemed to have forfeited their right to feminine protection within the private sphere by resorting to crime. Respectable women were expected to follow the model set by the previous Governor's wife, Eliza Arthur, and occupy an extremely circumscribed female world. Jane Franklin rejected the boundaries placed upon the world of respectable femininity, and threatened to enter the male world herself. Such an upset to the established order of things could not be tolerated. Dangerous as she was as support and ally to John Franklin, she appeared even more dangerous when represented as a woman manipulating her weak-willed husband in order to take power on her own account. And there were a number of ways in which Lady Franklin seemed to represent a significant challenge to the continuation of male supremacy in Van Diemen's Land. Queen Victoria had ascended the throne in 1837, and Jane Franklin's apparent dominance at a time when the British empire was adjusting to its first female monarch in well over a century may have focused some unspoken uneasiness about female rule. It is tempting to speculate, too, that her passionate desire to rid the island of snakes (she offered a shilling per head for every snake killed, until persuaded out of the scheme by the argument that convicts were neglecting their work in order to earn this easy money) was recognised as a symbolic castration, which threatened an almost entirely masculine society. Certainly her scheme provoked an extraordinary degree of ridicule and bitter hostility. In 1839, for example, a valentine was sent to her which consisted of a dead snake attached to a card, on which was written some insulting verses.[22]

But perhaps her greatest potential threat to male dominance was implicit in her criticisms of the assignment of convict women as domestic servants, under circumstances which offered little or no protection against enforced prostitution. Her interest in the lot of female prisoners was regarded as one of her 'most unforgivable crimes', and was condemned as indelicate and unwomanly. It was also successfully thwarted. As Jane lamented towards the end of her time in the colony: 'It has been the *one* object I have thought most about, & cared for most, since I have been in this Colony,—Yet what have I done—what have I been allowed to do?'.[23]

The perceived combination of energetic, clever wife and weak-willed, imbecilic husband was a lethal one, especially in a politically hostile environment. A governor who had not the intelligence, strength or experience to exercise command in his own right was a danger. Any individual who could dominate the governor would wield unrivalled power in the colony. The last years of the Franklins' administration were characterised by what can be seen as a struggle by the Colonial Secretary, John Montagu, to wrest this power from Lady Franklin.

In her efforts to clear the island of snakes, Jane had overlooked the real serpent in her midst. In 1839 Montagu had been described by Machonochie's wife as

> that snake in the grass, sleek, smooth & slippery . . . like many noxious animals he has the power of soothing & fanning his victims to sleep, never attacking openly or boldly . . . But from close & repeated examination, it is found he possesses *invisible* tentacula, which come from many quarters, puncturing, & injuring the victim, gradually destroying & undermining its character.[24]

A restless, ambitious man, Montagu had been tied during Arthur's administration by his many obligations to the Governor, and by Arthur's strict control of government. With Franklin's arrival, the relationship between Colonial Secretary and Governor changed. Montagu was quick to perceive Franklin's readiness to rely on advice, and assumed that it would be a simple matter to extend his power by gaining ascendancy over Franklin's mind. As he wrote later, Franklin's 'inaptitude for Public Business and his inexperience in the affairs and Science of Government could not be concealed. In fact his own frank admissions satisfied everyone upon these points'.[25] When Franklin dismissed his private secretary, Alexander Maconochie, Montagu's victory seemed assured. But at this point Jane's willingness to act as ally and adviser as well as wife threatened Montagu's plans. It increasingly seemed that Lady Franklin, and not he, would gain the ascendancy he coveted.

It is not clear how soon Montagu decided that Lady Franklin was the chief obstacle to his ambition. In the early years, although aware of her interest in the work of government, he did not openly censure it. Indeed, he discussed official correspondence with her, and on one occasion after a long discussion of transportation asked her to write down for him her views on the idea of making Tasmania the only penal colony and the probable impact of this on ideas for representative government. Lady Franklin did so, and Montagu conveyed a message of thanks and approval through Sir John. He also, it seems, kept her notes and later made use of them as evidence of her interference in government policy.[26] This incident can be read as the serpent tempting Lady Franklin with knowledge and power, and keeping the evidence for future reference, or it could have been fortuitous: he may have kept the notes because they genuinely appeared to him to express valuable opinions, and only later decided to put them to a different use.

Montagu's appearance of friendliness vanished after his return from two years' leave in 1841. One of his first actions was effectively to obstruct the founding of a boys' college, a favourite scheme of both the Franklins, which had seemed to be well on the way to fulfilment before his return. Later he argued that Lady Franklin had so resented his hostility to the project that she determined to bring about his dismissal.

It seems, rather, that he was attempting to bring about her political demise. In this endeavour he faced a particular difficulty. As a wife, Lady Franklin was a dangerous enemy, and difficult to vanquish. She could not, like Maconochie, be dismissed from office: she was a permanent fixture in Van Diemen's Land so long as Sir John remained there. Montagu had two options, and he tried each in turn. The first was to attempt to undermine Sir John's trust in her as confidante. The second, more radical, step was to bring about Sir John's recall, so that he would take his menacing wife back with him to England. Had Lady Franklin proved easier to suppress, it is unlikely that Montagu would have instigated Sir John's recall: his aim would have been to assert power in the colony through the governor. As Lady Franklin truly wrote, 'Woe to that poor woman if *the man who wishes to rule her husband* suspects she thwarts him in his design'.[27]

Initially, Montagu hoped to persuade Sir John that his wife was taking an improper part in administrative matters. His opportunity came in October 1841 when Sir John reconsidered a decision to dismiss the district medical officer in Richmond, Dr Coverdale, for negligence. Franklin was persuaded by a petition from Richmond residents that his previous judgement had been excessively harsh, and agreed to Coverdale's reinstatement. Montagu not only objected to this action, but suggested that the agitation in Richmond had been stirred up by Lady Franklin who, he claimed, had instigated the petition. He protested against what he described as her interference in affairs of state. Lady Franklin later denied the charge.

> The whole was a chimera of his own imagination, though had it been true that I had tried to save Sir John from persisting in an act which his own conscience told him was harsh if not unjust, I do not think I should have committed the blackest act which a wife, even a Governor's wife, ever was guilty of.[28]

Unfortunately for Montagu's ends, his attempts to undermine Sir John's confidence in his wife foundered: Sir John had been trusting his wife for years. In Jane's account, he went to her immediately after the interview, 'much excited and disgusted with Mr. Montagu', and asked straight out

> whether I had or had not said the particular thing attributed to me and which as far as he could discover was the sole cause of the suspicions against me. I perceived as well as Sir John had that Mr. Montagu's real errand was to strike a blow at me—blow of revenge for the past, and one which should paralyse me for the future—all this he hoped to effect by insinuating suspicions into Sir John's mind about me, but he never intended Sir John to communicate them. I gave Sir John the simple denial which he expected from me.[29]

And that was that. Montagu had perhaps fancied himself as Iago, but Franklin would not play Othello for him, and certainly Lady Franklin was no Desdemona. Sir John, like Jane, recognised that 'Mr. Montagu's object in denouncing her to me was to create distrust in my mind respecting her, and to destroy my confidence not only in her discretion but in her uprightness'. Sir John saw this attack as a private one, relating to his marriage, and at first believed that 'however destructive Mr. Montagu's proceedings were of all domestic intercourse or social confidence, yet the public need not have had any cognizance of the matter'. Montagu's aim, however, was to make this split as public as possible, and gain broad support for his criticism of Lady Franklin. He made some public statements about the impossibility of social intercourse between the Montagus and any inmate of Government House, including Franklin's private secretary. He said that neither he nor Mrs Montagu could enter the house of Lady Franklin, 'except himself upon *command* of Sir John'. At the same time he interpreted Franklin's request that all intercourse between them must thenceforth be strictly official to mean that he should no longer sort or comment on any administrative matters sent for Franklin's attention, claiming that such comment had been an act of friendship and not part of his official duties. This increased the governor's administrative burden to the point that government ground to a halt, ensuring wide public scrutiny of events. Finally, Montagu apparently used his contacts with one of the colonial papers to air versions of his attack on Lady Franklin.[30]

The Van Diemen's Land Chronicle, which appears to have been run under Montagu's patronage, published his version of the Coverdale case, and stuck to the story even though a number of people who had been involved with the petition denied that Lady Franklin had had anything to do with it. Montagu, despite his official position, which obliged him to support the Governor, remained publicly on terms of intimacy with the editors of the *Chronicle*. Eventually, Sir John felt obliged to write to Montagu on the subject, calling his attention to 'the scurrilous articles' against himself and his family which had appeared in the *Chronicle*, and enquiring 'whether he had taken any steps to uphold under such circumstances the dignity of my government'.[31] Montagu's reply was so insolent that Sir John, feeling that he could not retain Montagu as Colonial Secretary 'without detriment to the public service and dishonour to myself', suspended him from office.

Lady Franklin's part in this event, except as the focus of the 'scurrilous articles', was minimal. But she was soon to assume centre-stage again, placed there once more by Montagu. Several days after his suspension Montagu took a step which even his strongest supporters were to condemn when they finally heard of it. In a move which demonstrated that to a degree he believed in his comments about Lady Franklin's ascendancy over her husband, he pleaded with her to intercede for him. Already beginning to feel sorry for him, she did make an effort to encourage Sir John to modify his stance, and also offered Montagu some advice on a letter of apology which he planned to send. Montagu was later to assert that the intercession had been initiated by her. He claimed that through an intermediary, Dr Turnbull, she had offered to bring about a reconciliation if he agreed to two specified conditions, one of which was that he would support the building of the boys' college. When he nobly refused to be influenced by this attempt, Lady Franklin informed him through Turnbull that she 'would not depart from that condition, and that [his] suspension must take place'.[32]

This event, although at first it was kept secret, became central to Montagu's case of appeal against his suspension. He had been unable to persuade Sir John to exclude Lady Franklin from his counsels, but he now turned to his second strategy, which was to convince the colonial authorities in Britain of Franklin's unfitness to govern. In this endeavour, for the purpose of which he returned to England soon after his suspension, he was assisted by Sir John's very refusal to lessen the confidence he placed in his wife. Montagu suggested to the Secretary of State for the Colonies, Lord James Stanley, that it was essentially Lady Franklin, not Sir John Franklin, who had suspended him, because she had seen him as an obstacle to her outlandish plans for changes in the colony. This in one blow suggested Sir John's weakness and incompetence, indicated the unjustness of the suspension, and provided some evidence for the charge of interference which Montagu had made against Lady Franklin. Montagu's account of events was vehemently denied by Dr Turnbull, who wrote: 'I *never* stated that Lady Franklin would effect the reconciliation upon two conditions, and I *never* proposed to you the conditions which you have recorded. I would have cut off my right hand sooner.'[33] But it was Montagu's version of events which received a hearing in England.

Apart from this one event, in which he misrepresented matters grossly, Montagu had little in the way of concrete charges to bring against Lady Franklin. He took refuge in a chivalric, and very convenient, reluctance to bring a lady's name under the public eye.

> I have been unwilling to recount the devices it was well known to myself and others Lady Franklin resorted to, to make it appear that Public business was impeded, and that there was a public misunderstanding between Sir John Franklin and me, after I had mentioned her name to him on the 24th October, upon Dr. Coverdale's restoration. Nor do I desire to expose the attempts she had evidently made to hold me responsible for acts performed through her instrumentality. Some of these attempts extending even to Newspaper Articles. Nor will I allude to her interference in Public matters beyond what is necessary for my own exculpation.[34]

His avowed coyness on the subject did not prevent Lady Franklin's name from being brought into public discourse, and even forced Sir

John, despite a far more genuine reluctance, to include references to his relationship with his wife both in his explanatory letters to Lord Stanley and in the narrative of the events of the last years of his administration which he published soon after his return to England. Jane Franklin, too, was forced to reflect upon her relationship in letters to family and friends. Although this reflection and open discussion was obviously painful to both parties at the time, it has provided us with invaluable evidence about the public relationship of two private people in colonial society.

Montagu had not succeeded in persuading Sir John that Jane was deliberately exerting an undesirable influence over him. He was much more successful in persuading the English authorities that Sir John was a weak-willed husband, subservient to the will of his wife, allowing her to write all his despatches because he was too illiterate to write them without her help, and generally displaying himself as the obstinate imbecile that Montagu represented him to be. It was a persuasive picture, and Stanley fell for it. The despatch in which he recalled Sir John made little attempt to hide his contempt. In August 1843 Franklin was replaced by his successor before he had received official notification that Lord Eardley-Wilmot was on his way to the colony. The Franklins vacated Government House and spent some months visiting parts of the colony where they had been happiest. They did not leave until November 1843, when they were sent off with mass demonstrations of support and sorrow at their departure. They had come into bitter conflict with the rulers of the colony, in government and the media, but both husband and wife had won the respect and liking of many of the people of Van Diemen's Land. Lady Franklin received a prominent share of the respect and gratitude expressed in various public addresses. Whether hostile or friendly, the public had seen her as a central aspect of Franklin's administration, and were conscious always that they were dealing with a partnership and not an individual.

When the Franklins returned to England, Sir John set about lobbying for another Arctic command, with a desperation which he had never before shown. This is usually attributed to his belief that his professional reputation had been shattered by the version of his command in Van Diemen's Land which Stanley had accepted. In Fitzpatrick's words, he was driven 'by a blind urge to vindicate himself, to prove to himself and all the world that he was not a failure'.[35] Frances Woodward says he 'wanted his name cleared publicly and at once'; he wanted 'an acknowledgement that he had not betrayed his trust'.[36] It is possible also that he wanted a vindication of his masculinity, which had also suffered during his governorship. As the leader of various Arctic expeditions which had had to battle against nature's odds for survival, or as a naval commander in the Mediterranean, where his diplomatic as well as naval skills were frequently called upon, his masculinity had never come into question. But in his first 'domestic' appointment it had suffered considerably.

He had found the cares of government oppressive, and had leaned heavily on the support of his wife. He had seen that support publicly portrayed as interference, and himself represented as weak, and by implication unmanly, a henpecked husband unable to assert authority over his wife—worse, asking her aid. He had found himself, for the first time in his life, being the stay-at-home, while Jane was free to travel, making a name for herself (for good or bad) as a bold and intrepid explorer. His public image was constantly shadowed by that of his wife. Even his recall was dominated by arguments about the appropriateness of her behaviour, not his. She was the agent, he the dupe. Sir John asserted that the general object of criticisms in the hostile press was 'to excite hatred and contempt for my government and myself', while the suggestion of Lady Franklin's 'malign influence' was a 'special' object, 'subservient and tributary to the other'.[37] But the bitterness of the hostility expressed against Lady Franklin by Montagu and others raises the possibility that they engineered Franklin's recall as the only means of ridding the colony of this pestilent woman. Even as a public enemy, he was overshadowed by his wife. So damaged was his masculine image by his colonial experience that a joke was current in social circles after his recall: that the reason why he and Jane were childless was that 'his members got frost-bitten when he went to the North Pole'.[38] Perhaps there was an unspoken thought that they had been frozen by his over-virile wife.

There were many reasons why the Arctic was an appropriate place for Sir John to recover his lost masculinity. His aim was to cleave a passage through the icy mistress which had been his first love. Conquest of the polar regions had in the past earned him homage and veneration of his skills, strength and endurance. Perhaps he also remembered that last time he had set off on an Arctic expedition his first wife had died, and he may have sought—not Jane's actual death, but the death of that aspect of her which had dominated him

Sir John Franklin, portrait by Thomas Phillips, 1828

and sapped his masculinity in the past few years. Or perhaps the public world of politics and the private world of marriage became so inextricably mixed in his mind that both represented a confining, domestic world, and he yearned for the unrestricted spaces, the freer air, of the polar regions and the world of men.

What he found was death, and a death which could be popularly constructed as that of a heroic, manly man, trapped in the Arctic wastes and slowly starving in the interests of exploration. Through his death he restored to Jane Franklin a public role of devoted wifehood, essentially feminine. For years after his expedition failed to return, Jane persisted in lobbying governments and individuals, and herself providing private funds, to send expedition after expedition off after her husband, at first to rescue him or any of his band if at all possible, later simply to establish beyond all doubt the fact of his death, and to prove that he had indeed conquered the North-West Passage he had been so determined to find. It was twelve weary, anxious years from the time the expedition set out before Jane learned at last the date of her husband's death, in June 1847. During those years she earned a reputation as a devoted wife and widow which was to banish her previous reputation as eccentric, overbearing and interfering. She was once again the wife in the wings, waiting and watching with ever-diminishing hope for the return of her adventurous, active, tragic-heroic husband.

A marriage of opposites: Charles Joseph and Sophie La Trobe

Marguerite Hancock

In his youth, Charles Joseph La Trobe described himself as 'a gentleman in search of the picturesque'.[1] It was a pursuit which took him to foreign countries as the tutor and companion of a young Swiss count, and would provide the material for a series of travel books in which he called himself 'the Rambler'. It also brought about his meeting with the woman he would marry: Sophie de Montmollin. For Sophie, marriage meant a disruption from the protected environment of her large patrician family. She would follow her husband dutifully to the other side of the world when he was appointed Superintendent of the Port Phillip District, but she would never share his enthusiasm for travel. Theirs was a marriage of opposites: he was active, energetic, full of health and vigour; she was passive, retiring and inclined to be unwell. Marriage might have provided the restless Charles Joseph La Trobe with a sense of purpose, but not with the urge to settle down. His continuing wanderlust caused his wife much loneliness and anxiety, at the ultimate cost of her health.

In October 1824, the 23-year-old Charles Joseph La Trobe arrived at Neuchâtel, a quiet town on the shore of Lake Neuchâtel, near the French border of Switzerland. He had come to take up his duties as a tutor to the family of the Comte de Pourtalès, who had retired to Neuchâtel after a distinguished career in the French army. La Trobe would have suited his employer in several ways. Although he considered himself 'above all an Englishman',[2] he was, like Frédéric de Pourtalès, of Huguenot descent. He was also a member of the Moravian church, which encouraged personal piety, moral discipline and self-abnegation. The church was well known for its excellent non-denominational schools, and La Trobe had taught at a boys' boarding school run by the Moravian Brethren near Manchester. There was another Moravian school near Neuchâtel, and the Comte de Pourtalès would have been familiar with its high standard of teaching. La Trobe himself seems to have been anxious for the change: the death of his mother, after a series of personal crises, appears to have tipped the balance in favour of his leaving England.

Included as one of the household, the young tutor made the acquaintance of Frédéric-Auguste de Montmollin and his wife, Rose-Augustine de Meuron, who, as members of the intermarried 'noblesse' of Neuchâtel, were cousins of the Pourtalès family. M. de Montmollin was a counsellor of state, as were his father, grandfather and great-grandfather before him. After the Congress of Vienna, Neuchâtel had been simultaneously a canton of the Swiss confederation and a principality ruled by the King of Prussia. Accordingly, M. de Montmollin represented his canton at the Swiss Diet and served as a chamberlain at the Prussian court. His ancestral home, adorned with gargoyles, was on the market square of Neuchâtel.

Sophie, the ninth of the Montmollins' sixteen children, was fifteen years old when La Trobe first arrived at Neuchâtel, and twenty-six before he proposed to her. Their courtship, once it had begun, was interrupted each summer when Sophie left Neuchâtel for Jolimont, the country home of the Pourtalès family, and La Trobe took up his alpenstock and set out on his annual walking tour of the Alps. The nature of his work allowed him the freedom of long summer holidays, in which he took intense enjoyment. He was independent and energetic, a mountaineer who preferred to make his climbs without using a guide. Periods of solitude in the open air, away from the problems of everyday life, would always be important to him.

His love of nature was not simply the admiration of picture-postcard scenery but the informed enthusiasm of a student of natural science. Essentially, he saw his love of the natural world as an expression of his love of God. He saw the hand of the creator in all things: gazing in awe, exhilarated by the mountains, glaciers and lakes before him, his response was 'to adore and glorify the Creator of heaven and earth . . . in the presence of these stupendous and magnificent monuments of his power'.[3] But equally, when examined in this temper of mind, I have seldom held a flower in my hand, which I did not think curious and beautiful enough to have bloomed in paradise; and never returned the insect or reptile to its bed of leaves, without a feeling that the link that binds me to every living thing had become strengthened, and my sympathy towards the subject of my investigation excited and increased.[4]

La Trobe spent three years in Switzerland and then went away, probably to write and supervise the publication of his first and most successful book, *The Alpenstock; or, Sketches of Swiss Scenery and Manners*. This account of his first two summers in Switzerland was published in London in 1829. He spent the next summer travelling in the Tyrol, and then accompanied his pupil, Albert de Pourtalès, on a tour of Scotland and Ireland. His second book, *The Pedestrian: a Summer's Ramble in the Tyrol*, was the result.

The private journal on which this book was based shows that he was beginning to feel dissatisfied with his peripatetic way of life:

Supposing the words addressed to me, 'What dost thou here Elijah?' I have but a very sorry answer to give—Lord, I am on my road to the Tyrol & mean to write, & paint, & botanise, & amuse myself as well as I can, & perhaps shall publish and then—pshaw this is humiliating & leads me to say internally—well! I almost hope that, much as I love this kind of live [sic] & the pursuits with which I enliven it, this will be the last summer of the kind. I have travelled enough in this manner, enough to satisfy ordinate desires, & if I do travel & spend my strength in future years in this maner [sic], I pray God that I may have nobler aims and nobler purposes!—such as will not leave me to sit down & think as I have, & I fear may yet have to think during the course of this summer— 'Alas—I have spent my strength for nought!'[5]

Perhaps it was in this frame of mind that he began to contemplate marriage. Even so, the next spring he and Albert set out together on an extensive tour of the United States, Canada and Mexico which was to last a little more than two years. As they embarked at Le Hâvre, they made the acquaintance of Washington Irving, who was returning to his native America after seventeen years in Europe. He befriended them, and they travelled together for six months after arriving in New York. Irving later published a description of La Trobe which is invariably quoted by his biographers:

He was a man of a thousand occupations; a botanist, a geologist, a hunter of beetles and butterflies, a musical amateur, a sketcher of no mean pretensions; in short, a complete virtuoso; added to which he was

76   For Richer, for Poorer

>an indefatigable, if not always a very successful, sportsman. Never had a man more irons in the fire; and, consequently, never was a man more busy or more cheerful.[6]

This portrait is meant to be positive, but read in the light of the subject's own earlier words of self-doubt, it gives an impression of dilettantism, of a young man keeping busy in order to be cheerful. As if in illustration, Albert de Pourtalès drew a caricature of his tutor galloping across the prairies, standing on his horse's back like a circus performer with his coat-tails flying out behind him, drawing intently in his sketchbook.

La Trobe returned to England in the summer of 1834, where he stayed with his father and unmarried sister, Charlotte, at their home in Manchester. By the following spring, his next book, *The Rambler in North America*, was ready to be published, in two volumes. At the end of May he left again for Neuchâtel.

His journal shows that he had a definite object in mind, although he was in a state of some confusion. On 25 June he wrote: 'Mme C. [perhaps a chaperon] and S. arrived. Dont know what to think. Am like a ship lying at anchor but with a spring on its cable ready to make off at a moment's notice.' He spent the first week of July at Jolimont, then one evening went to Neuchâtel 'to follow up M. de Montmollin'. He missed him then and the following morning, but found 'her—nearly out this morning' and concluded that day's entry in his journal with 'I can think of n. but S.'. A week later he spent 'two or three sweet hours with S.' which was perhaps when he proposed, for by the next day he wrote that his mind was

>made up to the justice of setting S. at liberty by telling her father . . . In spite of overwrought state of mind & body off at 6 for La Prise—see and break the matter to Mme de M. her affectionate kindness. Come back in better spirits and breakfast . . . return at noon to Jolimont. Au net the last 10 days the most important in my eventful life. If I get S. I know what I have in her, neither beauty nor wealth but—

He left this sentence unfinished, unable, even in his 'Private Memoranda', to express his deepest feelings in words. But from the agitation of his entries he was clearly in love, and anxious. Would he be acceptable to the family? If Sophie had no independent wealth, La Trobe, at thirty-four, had scarcely made his place in the world. Perhaps with three published works to his credit, he felt at last in a position to offer his hand. Although companionship was becoming a more important reason for marriage, no gentleman would have considered proposing until he was able to support a wife and family. Doubts about his acceptability must have tormented him. On 29 July he was 'very ill at my ease & unable to do anything'. But by the next day he was 'determined not to absent mys[elf] from Neuchâtel till matters are arranged . . . a day of disappointment— followed by one of great joy'. On 31 July the engagement was 'approved' and announced to the family. The banns were read in London, and the wedding took place in the British Legation at Berne on 16 September 1835 'according to the ceremonies of the Church of England'.[7]

Their honeymoon was spent at Jolimont, but after three weeks La Trobe received word that his father had suffered 'a severe attack' and they returned to England immediately. By the time they arrived he had 'rallied in a wonderful manner', and they decided to stay with him during the winter. In April Sophie La Trobe received news of her own father's death, which was followed closely by Mr La Trobe's death in May. By the next month they were in London, where La Trobe was seeing his latest book, *The Rambler in Mexico*, through the press. They returned to Switzerland to be with Mme de Montmollin soon afterwards.

It was at this time that the name of Charles Joseph La Trobe came to the attention of the Secretary of State for the Colonies, Lord Glenelg. Despite an apparent lack of qualifications for the task, La Trobe was asked to report to the British government on the administration and use of funds voted by Parliament for the education of the newly-emancipated slaves in the West Indies. Patronage was the key to preferment, and it seems likely that his name was put forward by a member of the evangelical, abolitionist circle of which both his father and the Secretary of State were members. To a favourable eye, La Trobe's experience was, if anything, in education, and his four published works demonstrated quite amply his powers of observation and description.

His wife was expecting their first child but, having accepted Glenelg's offer, he was forced to leave her at Neuchâtel while he sailed for Barbados at the beginning of March 1837. Agnes Louisa was born on 2 April. La Trobe felt his absence at such a time very keenly and, still at sea a week before the baby was born, wrote: 'I can hardly think of my wife without gulping & cannot see a woman with a baby in her arms even if it be black, brown or yellow without feeling my heart climb into my throat'.[8] There is no record of Sophie La Trobe's response to their separation.

With both a wife and a child to provide for, La Trobe applied himself single-mindedly, setting out on a demanding tour of inspection which continued until July 1838. Now his talents and energies, once so dispersed, were concentrated. He produced three reports on negro education in Jamaica, in the Windward and Leeward Islands, and in British Guiana and Trinidad. It seems that Glenelg was sufficiently impressed to appoint him, in January 1839, to the new position of Superintendent of the Port Phillip District of New South Wales.

This time his wife was not to stay behind, but faced the unpleasant prospect of taking her infant daughter on a four-month ocean voyage to a vast penal colony at the other end of the earth. There was a tradition of service to the state in her own family, and this appointment was the next step on her husband's career, which now seemed set in colonial administration. And to these sincerely religious people, an unlooked-for opportunity such as this must have been taken as a direction not to be ignored.

They left England on 24 March with Agnes, two servants and a prefabricated house, and arrived in Sydney exactly four months later. La Trobe called on his immediate superior, Sir George Gipps, Governor of New South Wales, who invited the La Trobes to dinner. 'Declined for her', La Trobe wrote in his journal, without giving the reason. He went alone to Government House where he joined the 'large military and naval party'. During dinner, the conversation turned to the 'overland journey' which Lady Franklin had taken from Port Phillip to Sydney earlier in the year. La Trobe found Lady Franklin's counterpart in Sydney, Lady Gipps, 'exceedingly pleasing and unaffected'.

The La Trobes stayed in Sydney for nearly eight weeks, changing hotels when the first became too expensive. They spent most evenings 'quietly at home', as Mrs La Trobe had become ill and was 'confined to bed' for some days. La Trobe called several times at Government House while his wife was indisposed, receiving Gipps's 'very clear & luminous' account of 'the state of things at P. Phillip'.[9] Sir George Gipps was ten years older than Charles La Trobe, a veteran of the Peninsular War, with infinitely more experience of colonial administration. La Trobe must have felt very conscious of the fact that, until then, his experience of authority had been limited to the schoolroom.

When Mrs La Trobe was up again they made an excursion together by steamer to Government House, Parramatta, and another to breakfast on the North Shore. They dined at Government House several times and Mrs La Trobe began to pay calls and go for drives. She 'made a friend of Mrs Willis', no doubt the wife of the future resident judge at Port Phillip, who was to be such a thorn in her husband's side during his term as Superintendent. La Trobe was sworn-in before the Governor and Executive Council early in September, and a week later he and his family and servants sailed for Melbourne.

The new Superintendent was received with rapturous speeches and declarations of loyalty from the people of Melbourne, but his wife began as she meant to go on and stayed quietly in the background.

In his first letter to Gipps, La Trobe wrote with some relief that 'Mrs La Trobe is well, thank God, in the midst of all our discomfort & confusion for we have not yet been able to get into our quarters'. A residence was not provided under the terms of La Trobe's appointment. His salary of £800 a year was to '"include house-rent and every other charge" (except forage)', but rather than rent, the La Trobes chose to have their prefabricated cottage erected on 'a suitable spot in the Government paddock' within a fortnight of their arrival. (The materials for a larger wooden house had been ordered before they left London, but despairing of ever being able to afford the high price of land in Melbourne, La Trobe had sold the consignment before it was landed.)

These makeshift conditions were not unusual in a new settlement: Phillip had lived in a prefabricated house when he first arrived at Port Jackson fifty years earlier. At a similar stage in Melbourne's history, Captain William Lonsdale, who had acted as administrator before La Trobe's arrival, was still living in his original wooden cottage, also in the Government paddock. (He and his family were to remain the La Trobes' closest neighbours.) The parsimony of the British government meant that the standard of viceregal accommodation in the Australian colonies usually lagged behind that of the wealthier settlers. In La Trobe's case, the lack of a residence was also a mark of his peculiar position as Superintendent of the Port Phillip District. Until he was appointed Lieutenant-Governor of the

Sophie La Trobe with her daughters Eleanora and Cecile, *c.* 1853

new colony of Victoria in 1851, La Trobe actually lacked viceregal status; when Gipps drew up a proposed order of precedence in 1842 he placed the Superintendent fourth, after the Chief Justice, the Commander of the Forces and the Bishop of Australia.

The fact that the La Trobes were squatting in the Government paddock embarrassed Gipps. He felt unable to propose the idea of an official residence on the Superintendent's behalf, but offered his support if he were to make an application to the Secretary of State. La Trobe decided not to pursue this suggestion; he wrote in rather martyred tones that if the Government did not consider a residence necessary, he would wait until he was 'supposed to deserve more'. Meanwhile he had spent a considerable sum on improvements and was naturally reluctant to abandon his investment. At length Gipps was persuaded to allow the land to be put up at auction, and the Superintendent bid successfully for his $12\frac{1}{2}$ acres on 10 June 1840, at the upset price, approved by Gipps, of £20 an acre. 'It was a good penny in his pocket', wrote James Graham, the young Melbourne merchant, 'for if it is worth sixpence it is worth £500 an acre . . .'[10] La Trobe knew he had a bargain, and was surprised and gratified by the courtesy of the crowd who, with the exception of a speculator from Sydney, did not force the price up by bidding against him, but hung back, and then cheered his success. Gipps doubted the lasting nature of their goodwill, and in a confidential letter to La Trobe he wrote in some panic that the entire transaction amounted to the acceptance of a gift, and that he should not now expect to be granted an official residence if he chose to keep the land. La Trobe defended himself strongly by return of mail, but wrote again more moderately the next day. He was by then on the road to Westernport where, he suggested, 'perhaps I think the more coolly as my wife & child are out of the way'.[11] La Trobe's concern for his family was noted by Graham, who had written that the Superintendent 'was prepared to go the length of £350 an acre' at auction 'rather than have Mrs La Trobe's comfort broken in upon again'. Clearly her happiness was of far greater importance to him than any dream of marble halls. Gipps replied to La Trobe conciliatingly. Although he regretted that the Superintendent should have been compelled to become 'a landholder within the limits of his Government', and that Crown land should have been sold at such a low price, he confirmed the purchase.[12]

Edward La Trobe Bateman's sepia and wash drawing of Jolimont's park-like setting: its light-coloured roof is visible just to the left of centre.

The La Trobes named their property 'Jolimont', after the house where they had spent their honeymoon. The new Jolimont lay north of the Yarra, just north-west of the site now occupied by the Melbourne Cricket Ground. They were delighted with their home: as early as March 1840 La Trobe wrote to his sister Charlotte that 'small as our establishment is, I assure you there is not a more comfortable, well regulated and more tasty one in this part of the world both without and within'.[13]

The tininess of Jolimont is emphasised today because it has been re-erected at the rear gate of the palatial Government House which was built for later governors in the 1870s. Originally, the house consisted of six small rooms: a drawing-room and bedroom separated by a hall running from front to back with a weatherboard dining-room added on at the side, and two minute closets behind the drawing-room. The wall panels were fitted together on raised foundations, clad with boards roofed with hardwood slabs; the roof and foundations were extended to create a porch for the front door and a verandah to shade the dining-room windows. These were enclosed by a trellis so that climbing plants and vines could be trained over them, and around the supporting posts, to provide more shade. The interior panels were grained (with the skilful use of a feather, pine could be made to resemble oak), and the upper window panes had pointed Gothic arches. Various outbuildings were added: a kitchen hut, stables and a greenhouse, and later extensions were made to the house, including another verandah for Mrs La Trobe's use and a dressing-room for her husband, which opened on to the garden, his particular interest.

Two servants were brought from England to run this small establishment, and another was hired direct from her immigrant ship in Sydney. The La Trobes seem to have had the usual problems in keeping their servants, but one was constant, and she must have been Mrs La Trobe's mainstay. Charlotte Pellet was nine years older than her mistress and had worked in Madame de Montmollin's household at Neuchâtel as a nurse. She left to marry in 1836, and a daughter, Rose, was born in the next year. But in 1840 she divorced her husband and returned to the de Montmollin family, who suggested that she go out to the La Trobes in Australia as housekeeper. Charlotte and Rose arrived in March 1841 and stayed with the family for the next thirteen years.

The La Trobes did not live in a viceregal residence and they did not entertain on a viceregal scale. At the end of their first year at Jolimont, La Trobe wrote to his friend, the publisher John Murray, that they lived 'in tolerable tranquillity, despite our pre-eminence, in a pretty cottage about a mile out of Melbourne, which is really becoming a town'. Under the terms of his appointment, La Trobe did not feel obliged to live beyond his means in order to dispense hospitality to the people of Melbourne, and he did not expect his wife to act as an official hostess. 'As you will gather', he wrote to his sister, 'we live very retired, neither receiving nor giving general invitations and keeping as much in the background as possible. By degrees we shall get a choice of society about us. As long as my salary & appoint^t are what they are, I can never pretend to act the Governor & see company in Govt style, so the more quiet I keep the better'.[14] He expressed himself in stronger terms to Murray:

> I had the common sense to start at once with the determination that whatever my supposed position and liabilities might be, so long as Her Majesty's Government neither gave me a house nor the means of keeping an open one, I would not pretend to do so to please the little world

around me. A man with a fortune may spend it, and ruin himself, to please people, if he think proper; but having no fortune, I could not even do that.[15]

Under the circumstances, the barely adequate size of Jolimont worked to the La Trobes' advantage. With no wish to entertain on anything but an intimate scale, their tiny residence prevented lavish hospitality. On the infrequent occasions when the Superintendent held a ball or levée, the Government Offices in William Street served the purpose.

The La Trobes abhorred display: their tastes were simple and refined. This was not well received in Melbourne; it seems that from the beginning the Superintendent and his wife were expected to maintain a standard which reflected favourably the perceived importance of the community they represented. In 1848, members of the Melbourne Town Council composed a petition to Queen Victoria requesting La Trobe's removal for failing, among other charges, to keep up a standard suitable to his position. 'The Town Council votes the Superintendent a bore', he wrote to a friend in Launceston, 'the cause of all the mischief that has taken place in the world to the S. of the Tropic of Capricorn for the last 9 years, or something like it—and request Her Majesty to turn him out neck and crop ... One does get a little tired of all this—but after all must stick to it, & do one's duty as well as may be'.[16]

The La Trobes certainly invited people to Jolimont, but to small dinner parties for perhaps half a dozen guests, or to musical evenings, not large receptions. La Trobe wrote later that on average they had guests to dinner once a week. In that male-dominated society, Mrs La Trobe, like other Melbourne hostesses, frequently presided at a table that was surrounded entirely by men. After attending one such 'gentlemen's dinner', the newly arrived squatter and future judge, Robert Williams Pohlman, wrote in his diary: 'No Lady other than Mrs La Trobe—is said that Ladies not invited usually by them'. No doubt a little offended because his own wife was not included, Pohlman failed to realize that the La Trobes' apparently exclusive policy took practical difficulties into account. In the early years of Melbourne, women suffered considerable difficulties when travelling at night on unlit, unmade roads. This was borne out some weeks later, after Mrs Pohlman had made the La Trobes' acquaintance and accepted an invitation to tea. The Pohlmans walked to Jolimont, but the oppressive December weather broke while they were inside

Front view of Jolimont by Edward La Trobe Bateman, who was Charles La Trobe's cousin. This drawing shows the house in its final form, with all the additions made to the original prefabricated cottage over the years. Although it has been dated 1854, the three figures in the garden, who seem to be Sophie La Trobe and two of her children, suggest that it was made in the previous year for the sake of his lonely cousin.

the house, and their host had to escort them home, chivalrously protecting Mrs Pohlman with his umbrella.[17] Georgiana McCrae recorded dining at Jolimont on only one occasion in her journal, when she was also inconvenienced by the weather. She wrote that after the meal there was 'a sudden change of wind and so we had to wade across the hollow & only got home at half past ten'.[18] Her destination was Bourke Street, which she had left for Jolimont five hours earlier. An indefatigable hostess herself, her own dinner guests in the early 1840s were almost exclusively male. Towards the end of the decade balance was restored to the La Trobes' table, and married couples such as the new Bishop of Melbourne and his wife were invited regularly. The La Trobes were not constrained by the protocol which prevented later governors and their wives from dining at private homes, and accepted hospitality within a circle which could be described as 'professional, with squatting interests'. Mrs La Trobe's personal friends were drawn from the married women within this circle.

Although gentlemen's clubs were established in Melbourne at a very early date, gentlemen's wives made social contact through 'morning calls'. These short, formal visits of about twenty minutes' duration were usually paid between two and four o'clock in the afternoon, despite their name, so as not to disturb household routine. English practice was preserved in Melbourne, including the ritual of leaving cards, but it seems that in the case of the Superintendent's wife, the usual order of precedence was reversed, and newcomers made the initial call at Jolimont. Accordingly, a fortnight after her arrival in Melbourne, Mrs McCrae paid her first call on Mrs La Trobe, whom she found '*tres aimable pour moi*, et tres myope!'. They spoke in French as Mrs McCrae had expected. 'In the habit of speaking French continually' herself from the age of nine, she had found that her fellow First Cabin passengers on the voyage to Australia had occupied their mornings with the study of '"Cobbetts French grammar" . . . as it was supposed that Madame La Trobe could not speak English'.[19] In fact her letters show that, despite an occasional awkward phrase, Mme La Trobe's command of English was perfect.

It was her fragile health, rather than any difficulties with the language, which limited Sophie La Trobe's enjoyment of social engagements. Georgiana McCrae, one of her close circle, referred to the '*affreux* headaches' which confined Madame to her bed. La Trobe was also conscious that his wife was not robust, and frequently expressed his concern at times of stress and upheaval. He wrote lightly, however, to John Murray about the reason for her problems.

> Mrs. La Trobe has not been over strong since her arrival in these regions of the globe, although enjoying good general health. I am not quite sure that standing with the head downwards (as you know we are obliged to do here) suits the female constitution, though one gets wonderfully used to it after the first month's trial.[20]

Probably childbearing did nothing to improve her health. Three more children were born in Australia: Eleanora (Nelly) in 1842; Cecile the next year and Charles on Christmas Day 1845. It seems very likely that she was expecting another baby in 1848. La Trobe, on his way to Portland in March of that year, ended a letter to this wife with: 'What a pity that you cannot with[t] inconvenience anticipate next August'.[21] While he was still away, Mrs La Trobe had a fall from a carriage, with grave, though unspecified, effects on her health: she had probably suffered a miscarriage with complications. In September she told Nelly and Cecile's teacher that she had 'been very ill for nearly 4 months most of which time I was confined to my bed, into the house on the sofa. I have, been, thank God, much better for some time but I have not as yet recovered my normal health and do not know whether I shall ever recover it'.[22]

She continued to be plagued by neuralgic headaches. In 1850, during the Separation celebrations, she asked Georgiana McCrae to take her place at the official opening of Prince's Bridge. It was a public holiday and if she stayed at home the servants would be free to take it; her head was aching and she wanted to avoid the 'cannonading'. Her friend agreed, and, dressed in Mrs La Trobe's jacket trimmed with black Australian swansdown and her own grey silk bonnet 'like Madame's', she took her place in the carriage and acknowledged the greetings of the crowd.[23]

In marked contrast to his wife's avoidance of outdoor activity, La Trobe continued to revel in expeditions and adventures. As Superintendent of Port Phillip, he could take up his old rambling habits with a new sense of purpose. Although expeditions to acquaint himself with the District and its problems were neither required of him as Superintendent nor funded by the Colonial Office, La Trobe frequently set off at his own expense, 'outfit and all', to enjoy dangers and camaraderie in a male world. During his fifteen and a half years in Australia he recorded ninety-four journeys. Some of these were summer holidays with his wife and children, two were trips to Sydney and Hobart on official business, but the majority were taken on horseback with one or more companions. Captain Henry Pulteney Dana, a friend from England and the commander of the native police force, often accompanied him. Most trips lasted three to five days, but some, to distant places such as Portland, Gippsland, Cape Otway or the Murray River, could keep him away for over a fortnight. He experienced occasional hazards, but returned from all his trips unharmed except for a wound in his side which continued to trouble him. At his first 'rencontre with natives' he found them 'only half friendly'; a boat trip to Westernport Bay nearly ended in disaster; rain followed by snow and the threat of heavy floods turned him back on an excursion to Dandenong. But clearly he loved these excursions, which provided both the joy of discovery and the opportunity to get away from domestic life and the burdens of office and let off steam in congenial company. Towards the end of his time in Australia he told Ronald Campbell Gunn, one of his travelling companions, that

> I have laughed heartily at your apologetic misgivings lest you may occasionally have forgotten in the lighthearted harum scarum individual trotting by your side the representation of Royalty under sign manual. I am sure you have no sin to repent of; on the contrary, I owe you thanks that your character & humour was such as to encourage me to unbutton & unlace without restraint, whenever my humour prompted—and allow me to act up to my own belief that even the wise man who dare not & cannot play the fool sometimes is a great ass—.[24]

In many ways Sophie La Trobe embodied the idea of the early Victorian lady: retiring, delicate, attached to the comforts and security of home, and frequently confined to her sofa. Perhaps anxiety caused her frightful headaches, or perhaps La Trobe rode off so frequently to escape the atmosphere of ill-health at home. Certainly she worried: her husband's departures brought forth 'expressions of regret, anxiety & prayers for his safety', and his returns 'the most aff^t proofs of thankfulness to God & joy & contentment'. During his absences he wrote letters and sent them by any means available: affectionate and reassuring letters, often warning her of a change in plan which would delay his return.

> My dear wife
> You will have seen from my notes written en route that it would be quite impossible for me to be back with you quite as early as you were led to hope. For I could not stop less than two days in Portland, and then Sunday today intervening I could of course not get off before tomorrow mor^g. So I am very glad to get your brief note of this day's mail—and to see that you are all well.
> Tomorrow I start early for Port Fairy 50 miles—& the next day get on to Warrnambool—& a little further perhaps on my road home—I am pretty [well supplied] with horses & shall do what I can to be with you to dinner on Thursday—b^t that can only be the case if I meet with no check whatsoever—so dont be astonished if I do not see you till Friday. People are kind and complimentary here—& I wish you were with me. I send a note to each of the little girls & five kiss[es] to Charley.
> You will I am sure think of y^r old husband tomorrow.
> Good bye dearest
> C. J. La Trobe[25]

The acknowledgement of her concern was not allowed to limit his freedom of action: '. . . all I can say is cherie if I am not back on Sat^y night—you need not be anxious—for I may not find it possible—& I had better not leave undone what I have to do—many hours after, I trust I shall not be, only say this in case that you may not imagine 1 000 000 horrors'.[26]

Sophie La Trobe's life was not lived entirely at Jolimont. Although her husband could seldom persuade her to leave the children and accompany him on even his least demanding journeys, she seems to have enjoyed their family holidays by the seaside. The first was spent at Williamstown, where La Trobe rented a cottage from the harbourmaster for a fortnight at the end of 1841. He commuted from there to his office in Melbourne and to Jolimont, which was undergoing additions and repairs. By 1844 'some change during the hotter summer months appeared absolutely requisite' so they took rooms in the first huts erected at Shortland's Bluff (now Queenscliff) and built more as necessary. Mrs La Trobe and the children stayed there from February until April, La Trobe visiting when he could. This holiday 'was productive of so much pleasure' that they decided to make more permanent arrangements for the following year. A three-roomed cottage 'with verandah—& tents, & store & open cooking shed' was built 'on the highest ground over the North end of the Bluff—a charming situation'. La Trobe planned and constructed it himself, sending building materials across from the opposite shore on the lime boats which travelled constantly back and forth. He had it ready by the beginning of January, and Mrs La Trobe and the children stayed until late March, joined by La Trobe whenever possible. He went to extraordinary lengths to be with them:

> I was accustomed to go to the Bluff ordinarily by steamer to Geelong & a ride of 20 m[iles] tho' occasionally the outward bound steamer afforded facilities. By getting off from the Bluff at 4 am & riding 20 m[iles] to Geelong before 7 & then getting on the morning steamer as I often did this & the following year I was often at my office at Melbourne in good time for dispatch of business. We had frequent visits.

They returned the next year, but in 1847 they were in Van Diemen's Land where La Trobe was Acting-Governor for four months, and in 1848 he had the cottage removed and re-erected at Jolimont, 'the distance and inconvenience being too great'.[27]

Early in 1845 the La Trobes faced the painful decision of whether to send their eldest daughter, Agnes, back to Switzerland for the sake of her education. They had worried for some time that she was being allowed to run wild in the parklike surroundings of Jolimont. Although at five years old she was 'a noble little girl . . . pretty . . . and full of talent' her father had also described her as being 'as wild as a march hare & giddy beyond all endurance'.[28] A Swiss governess, Mademoiselle Béguin, had joined the family, and Agnes had also

The La Trobes' holiday cottage, which was moved from Shortland's Bluff (Queenscliff) and re-erected at Jolimont when 'the distance & inconvenience' proved 'too great'

attended classes at the Mechanics' Institute in Collins Street, but it was thought best that she be with her grandmother and Aunt Rose in Neuchâtel. In April 1845, only weeks after her eighth birthday, she sailed on the *Rajah* in the care of Mrs Ferguson, the Captain's wife.

In the belief that such early separations were in their best interests, parents throughout the British empire made the sacrifice of sending their children home to school, sometimes never to see them again. After hearing of the La Trobes' decision, Gipps wrote comfortingly of his son's good progress at Eton: 'we know what it is to part with a child under such circumstances—but we know also that *we did right*, in sending our Boy home'.[29] Sons rather than daughters were usually sent: it was often thought that a girl could be educated adequately at home by a governess, or at a well-run local school, but a boy's education was the foundation of his career, and the great public schools of Britain laid a much firmer foundation than their nascent colonial counterparts.

It was nearly a year before her parents knew that Agnes had arrived safely. Her mother wrote to her for the first time in February 1846:

> Though we have had no letters as yet from you, my dearest little girl, we think you will be glad not to be too long without hearing from papa & maman—We know that the Rajah arrived in London on the 4th of October & we hope soon to receive letters from your own handwriting, & all the many details kind Mrs Ferguson promised me on you & all your doings. We know too that as far as Rio di Janeiro you have had dreadful stormy weather & we thank God with all our hearts to have preserved you amidst so many dangers—& I was glad to hear by a letter from Mrs Ferguson, to Uncle Peter that you had been very well & very cheerful—& a good obedient girl.—If you could only know dearest child how happy we are when we learn that you have been a good & docile child. I hope you will endeavour to be so always so that good aunt Rose & G^{d}maman may always be pleased with you, & report well of you.[30]

After Agnes had been away for five years, her mother feared that she would forget her parents in Australia 'who wish so much not to become strangers to their dear child whom they so tenderly love'.

She asked to be remembered to her friends and family in Switzerland: 'Oh! I should like, so, so much to see you all, if they only knew—'[31]

La Trobe finally submitted his resignation in December 1852, but was not free to leave the colony for over a year. They decided that Mrs La Trobe and the children, with Mademoiselle Béguin, would leave first, and wait for him at Neuchâtel. La Trobe took them to the ship and waited with them until they sailed on 25 February 1853. Charlotte Pellet stayed on at Jolimont to care for him, but he missed his family cruelly. In October a visit to Shortland's Bluff inspired him to write a long letter to his wife:

> I cannot forget that the last time I was here, it was with you my darling, & my dear children, & my heart is un peu gros—but I feel that I have so much to be thankful for on your account with respect to the voyage which you were then entering upon & I feel that no other feeling ought to be uppermost. I have never been at the Heads since we parted . . . you cannot imagine my dear wife how fully my mind has been occupied with you & my dear children. My dear wife yesterday & today I see you at every turn—on the beach on the hill, at the Lighthouse, at the gate of our pretty cottage—the children run way down the steep pathway to the sand & calling out papa Papa! as in times past at Point Lonsdale . . . In fact Jolimont itself is not more full of recollections—& perhaps these are the more vivid because I had some of my pleasantest days in Victoria here with you. May God bless you wherever you are.[32]

Sophie La Trobe may never have read this touching letter. Eight days before he was to leave Australia, La Trobe happened to see his wife's death notice in a London newspaper. She had died at Neuchâtel on 30 January 1854 of a disease of the liver, probably cancer. La Trobe was completely unprepared for this news. He had hoped that the long sea voyage and the reunion with her family in Switzerland would have restored her completely, but letters from their children confirmed the terrible report. Admidst the chaos of leaving the colony after almost fifteen years, it was an appalling shock. 'Poor Mr La Trobe felt deeply the loss of Mrs. La Trobe', wrote James Graham to a mutual acquaintance. 'You know he was a truly affectionate husband.'[33] Some years earlier, the usually reticent La Trobe had expressed his deepest feelings to an American cousin: 'I have to bless God for having led me to stop short in my wandering life for a short interval to form that connection which has been & is the source of so much joy to me under all times & circumstances'.[34]

In 1855 a memorial tablet to Sophie La Trobe, with a simple inscription composed by her husband, was sent from London at his expense to be placed in St Peter's, the parish church of the City of Melbourne. 'I think that she deserves to be remembered in the community of which she was so long a member', he wrote to a friend.[35]

When La Trobe decided to marry again, it was to his youngest sister-in-law, Rose de Meuron. She was a widow, twenty years younger than La Trobe, the same Aunt Rose who had cared for Agnes when she was sent home to Neuchâtel. Their marriage pleased the family, who found it a natural and sensible arrangment, but it was not without legal obstacles. Under English law, marriage to a deceased wife's sister was marriage within the prohibited degree, and therefore illegal. They were able to marry in Switzerland, on 1 October 1855, but only after the President of the Republic had ordered La Trobe to place a bond of 2500 Swiss francs in a Swiss

DEAD.
OUNLIFFE.—On the evening of the 4th inst., at his residence, 1, Upper Hyder-park-street, James Ounliffe, Esq., of 24, Lombard-street, aged fifty-six.
LA TROBE.—On the 30th ult., at Neûchatel, in Switzerland, at the residence of her mother, Madame de Montimollin Meuron, Sophie, the beloved wife of his Excellency Charles J. La Trobe, Lieutenant-Governor of the colony of Victoria, in the forty-fourth year of her age.

A detail from the *Morning Post*, 8 February 1854, showing Sophie La Trobe's death notice bank account. Apparently their successful circumvention of English law inspired many brothers and sisters-in-law to marry across the Channel. They had two daughters, Margaret and Isabelle.

La Trobe, whose eyesight was failing, was never given another official appointment. He was made a member of the Order of the Bath and given the minimum governor's pension which, with the sale of Jolimont, allowed him a modest retirement in England. After his death in 1875, his widow returned to Neuchâtel where she built a private chapel, 'l'Hermitage', in his memory.

The moral reformer and the imperial major: Caroline and Archibald Chisholm

Patricia Grimshaw

On 27 December 1830, Caroline Jones, a yeoman farmer's daughter from the village of Wootton, and Archibald Chisholm, a lieutenant in the Indian Army, were married in the Church of the Holy Sepulchre at Northampton, England, the church where Caroline had been christened twenty-two years before. Archibald was thirteen years her senior, with a career as a soldier already well established. He was of Highland Scottish origin from Knockfin, a Roman Catholic from an impoverished but 'respectable' family, who had followed his older brother into the Honourable East India Company Army and served in Burma from 1824 to 1826, and subsequently in Madras, India. Archibald's mother had died when he was six years of age, and he was reared by an aunt. Caroline had lost her father, William Jones, at the same age, but her mother, Sarah, had kept on the prosperous farm for herself and her large family, the oldest of whom married and settled in the district. Caroline's mother's household was a large, open and hospitable one, and Caroline had spent the years of her early maturity assisting with the concerns of kin and neighbourhood in this rural community.

The couple first met at a ball while he was stationed at the Northampton Barracks. Archibald was immediately attracted to the lively, tall, good-looking, red-headed Caroline and moved rapidly to indicate his interest in marriage: his return to his regiment in India might not be long delayed. Caroline was not so certain. She was an unusual young woman, who had responded in particular ways to certain influences in her childhood, stemming from the social dislocation of her district, and from religious reforming initiatives in the church. There had been stability in Caroline's own personal life, radiating from her mother's capable management of the household,[1] but around her there was evidence of much human misery arising from the industrial revolution. As machinery led to the concentration of manufacturing in factories, wage labour became widespread, and common land was enclosed, rural dwellers were moving to growing towns, and towns were becoming teeming cities. Wretched living conditions and near starvation wages caused destitution; hunger, epidemics and premature deaths were common occurrences. In the face of such need, the swelling ranks of the middle class were at first indifferent, attached as they were to the self-indulgent enjoyment of wealth. Evangelicals within the Church of England, led by such forceful figures as William Wilberforce and Hannah More, chided their fellows to develop a social conscience, and held up the fear of mass revolution if gentler change did not take place. And whence would come the model of reform? From no other place than the well-ordered, affectionate family, centre of the nation's moral values. From the decent family of breadwinning father, defender of the hearth, from the wife, keeper of its conscience, and carer of dutiful children, would radiate unselfishness to soften greed, and love to inspire peaceful resolutions of conflict. Women, chaste, faithful and steadfast, were to hold a key place in the rejuvenation of social relations, through their charitable acts, and their influence on men.

Sarah Jones, Caroline's mother, had introduced her daughters from childhood to notions of obligation to the poor and needy, as well as tolerance towards people of different faiths. The Jones home was always open to neighbours and travellers who needed food, or a bed for a short stay. That Caroline had developed an early social conscience was clear from her story of a game she played when not yet seven years of age. Sending impoverished people off to British colonies was an idea in the air, proposed even for the fledgeling convict settlement of New South Wales. Caroline practised some economic theory, as she later recalled in her own account of her early life. First she filled a wash-basin with water.

> I made boats of broad-beans; expended all my money in touchwood dolls; removed families, located them in the bed-quilt, and sent the boats filled with wheat ... back to their friends. At length I upset the basin,

which I judged to be a facsimile of the sea, spoiled a new bed, got punished, and afterwards carried out my plan in a dark cellar with a rushlight.[2]

In the same boat, interestingly enough, Caroline had placed a Wesleyan minister and a Catholic priest. Her parents were tolerant of religious difference in a period when this was far from usual. Indeed, a French Catholic priest, a refuge during the Napoleonic wars, had once found shelter in their home when few in the district would countenance assisting him. Tolerance of those of other faiths became an unusual feature of Caroline's public outlook in future years.

As she reached maturity, Caroline came to a conviction that she possessed a vocation for special, dedicated philanthropic endeavour. Had she been raised a Roman Catholic, she might well have pursued this vocation through the celibate life of the nun. As Florence Nightingale was later to complain, however, the Anglican Church encouraged no such single-minded devotion. But Caroline, having rejected several other suitors, found another way. When Archibald Chisholm proposed, she in turn offered an unusual bargain. She extracted a promise from him that, even as a married woman and an officer's wife, she should be free to engage in philanthropic work as energetically as she wished. She gave Archibald a month to consider: after all, she obviously had her heart set on something more than simple neighbourly charity, and she realised the bargain was an unconventional one. Archibald proved to be a match for her, and accepted.

Archibald himself was no stranger to the social misery Caroline witnessed, since the Highland tenant farmers in his own Scottish home were being displaced so that sheep could graze and a few landholders could prosper. Many poor Highlanders fled to the coast to find a living through the sea; some migrated to distant colonies. In addition, he had himself never experienced any conventional home life, and perceived no fixed boundaries between a wife's duties to husband and children and to the poor and needy. Archibald was to prove a singularly sympathetic husband, not only in his acceptance of such a condition on their marital relationship, but in the steadfast way he would uphold that promise for the duration of their marriage. It was a promise easier, perhaps, to honour because of the unusual geographical context of this British couple's married life.

Archibald's imperial involvement would provide the environment for his wife's life of reform. First he took her to Madras where he

Archibald Chisholm as a young officer in the 30th Madras Native Infantry

served in the East India Company regiment, and she first noted the anomalies resulting from concentration of single expatriate British men in foreign places. Next he took her to New South Wales for his furlough, and there she came into her own, as the needs of the colony and her personal convictions found a fortunate coincidence.

His long absences on military service gave her respectable, and financially sustained, periods of personal autonomy, and freedom from pregnancies. Retiring at a relatively early age on an army pension, Archibald was then free to give active assistance to his singular wife's causes. In the married partnership of Caroline and Archibald Chisholm, the concerns of gender and the concerns of empire neatly, and fortuitously, intersected.

On her wedding day Caroline presented herself to Archibald at the altar demurely clad in white, with orange blossom holding her veil. After the service, Archibald and Caroline travelled to Brighton where they lived in rented rooms, awaiting Archibald's recall to his regiment, which occurred within the year. Caroline was received into the Catholic Church, and wrote in her diary that she went frequently to the chapel to pray for her 'dear Archy' during the year she spent there before joining him in Madras in 1833. She recorded that she carried out a quantity of needlework during her lonely year: it was not an occupation that was to preoccupy her much in the future. On her arrival in Madras, the couple took up residence within the mile-square compound of Fort St George, where the army had its barracks, and married officers lived in separate quarters. Other officers' wives introduced Caroline to the life of leisure and the social round with which they filled their days. There were servants to supervise, tea parties to give with their gossip and pleasantries, summer vacations in the mountains to plan. An English woman, Lady Julia Maitland, wrote sarcastically of the life during her three-year stay at the Fort in the late 1830s. Even the horse, she joked, 'had a man and maid to himself—the maid cuts grass for him—and every dog has a boy. I enquired whether the cat had any servants, but I found she was allowed to wait upon herself; and as she seemed the only person in the establishment capable of so doing, I respected her accordingly'. Lady Julia found 'ladies all young and wizen, gentle-men all old and wizen'.[3] Now the wife of a captain, since Archibald was promoted on his return to active service, Caroline's status rose—but this was scarcely the style of life she had in mind for herself.

Caroline had not been long in Madras, therefore, when she took an extraordinary step: she began a school for soldiers' daughters, both English and those of mixed descent, in the predominantly Indian quarter of Black Town, outside the comfortable complacency of Fort St George. Caroline and Archibald moved into a house next to a building large enough to accommodate the girls who lived as well as learned under Caroline's watchful tutelage. Officers' wives were not expected to act so, although since donations from local benefactors for the school were not slow in coming, many other Europeans in Madras must have shared her concern.

Archibald's fellow officers warned that the couple would find themselves isolated socially from the officers' set, when they moved from the army barracks to the poorer quarters of Madras. There was the considerable fear also of contracting fevers in their new hot, cramped and overcrowded neighbourhood. Nothing daunted, and with Archibald's backing, Caroline established their school on a firm footing. She was in charge, with several servants to help with the work of caring for the numerous girls, and the girls themselves, young as they were, as useful assistants. According to Caroline, their fate, if left unschooled, appeared an unfortunate one: very early marriages, leading to impoverished and often brutalised lives; or prostitution within the soldiers' ranks, leading to ill health from venereal diseases and their accompanying infections. She saw one answer for these girls: a training that would provide, along with basic skills in reading, writing and arithmetic, the basis for their honest waged employment. They would learn the crafts of good housewifery, budgeting, thrifty shopping, keeping accounts, plain cookery, cleaning, ironing and washing. They would in this way develop a stronger sense of their own worth; they would have the capacity to earn an independent livelihood; they would attract suitors among the more respectable soldiers, and match their husbands' resource provision with household skills of equal value. Confronted by the social practices of an expatriate community which was predominantly male, she began to search for structural explanations for the problem of gender. Single girls and women needed honest work—men needed good wives. Women should exploit their utilitarian value, not their sexuality, for a living. Men should remain celibate as they awaited good, virtuous wives who would curb their otherwise ungoverned appetite for sexual adventures. She would think of this more extensively at the sight of early colonial society in New South Wales.

In the meantime, Caroline persisted in her goal, despite the absence of Archibald for a year, when he was sent inland to Vellore on military duties, and despite two pregnancies and births. In May 1836 in Madras she gave birth to a son, named Archibald after his father, and in September 1837, in the cooler air of the hills at

Hyderabad, a son William, named after her own father. (Caroline had very possibly experienced stillbirths before this time: she referred at the end of her life to giving birth to three dead babies as well as to the six living infants she eventually bore. It is likely that this occurred during this early phase of her marriage, since the birth of her first living child was five and a half years after their marriage.) In conducting a private school, Caroline was undertaking a utilitarian task, one not unknown among middle-class English women who needed to make money. The work could be carried out at home, with the school and teachers' domestic establishments intertwined. But this situation of the Chisholms had decided differences. In the usual English arrangement, a married woman so occupied would usually be widowed: if married, she was usually assisting a husband's teaching endeavour. In this case, Archibald had another waged occupation. In the usual private school, the pupils were of middle-class origin; here, the children were mixed-race and poor. In the usual private boarding school, the motive was making money; here the motive was philanthropy.

Caroline established, then, very early in her marriage, her right to an autonomous existence. This disregard of convention was sanctioned by an assertion of altruistic endeavour, assisted by the clear fact that the endeavour itself aimed at bringing girls firmly within the bounds of a decent ordered life in terms of middle-class criteria. Caroline established here a basis for their marriage that would also mark their choices in the future. She and Archibald shared little sense that a good marriage would involve a closed personal relationship played out in an exclusive private space. Their relationship would flourish, if flourish it did, not only amidst their own children, but with numerous other people lodging and visiting (servants and assistants, relatives and friends) and with the presence of the beneficiaries of philanthropic labour and benefactors. Marriage for both was, certainly, about affection, loyalty, devotion. It was about rearing well-cared for children who were honest, dutiful and obedient. But marriage was not about a tight, introverted environment for intense emotional bonds. Such a model of the marriage relationship was helpful for a married woman with children who had ambitions outside routine housewifely duties.

Archibald's occupation as an army officer removed Caroline from village life and thrust her on to a British imperial frontier. While he defended his country's hegemonic economic interests there, his wife

A contemporary portrait of Caroline Chisholm

turned her attention to reforming what she perceived as the anomalous gender practices of expatriate male enclaves. Hence Archibald's and Caroline's concerns nicely intersected. And their interests were to do so again, when Archibald, due for furlough, was released a little early because of ill health, and decided to spend his leave in New South Wales where the climate was considered favourable. (Another attraction of New South Wales to East India Company officers was that convict servants could be employed for no cost.) In March 1838, with their young sons, the couple left on the *Emerald Isle* for Sydney, which they finally reached in September.

They settled quite comfortably into a rented house in Windsor, with a housekeeper in train. Caroline gave birth to another son, Henry, the following July.

Early in 1840, when the baby was six months old, and the other boys two and three, Archibald and Caroline made another unusual decision about their relationship. Archibald was recalled to his regiment. Caroline decided to stay in Sydney alone, with their children. Sydney was undeniably preferable for English people, especially children; and even had they returned with Archibald to Madras, he might have had prolonged absences on active service. Yet one suspects that the driving force behind the decision arose from another source: Caroline's strong sense that there was work for her to do among the colonists of Sydney. Her first thought (she later told an Irish audience) was to begin a school somewhat on the lines of her Madras venture; 'but her husband, believing that she had some talent which she might devote to a useful object, said he knew her better than she did herself, and that emigration was her field. She followed his advice and acted accordingly, merely in obedience to him'.[4] According to Caroline, then, it was not merely Archibald's assent, but his active promotion of her career, that underwrote their decision to undergo this temporary separation.

It was five long years before the pair were reunited. In the meantime, Caroline became one of the most prominent figures in Sydney life. She was free for a useful spell from pregnancies and breastfeeding; her husband's salary underwrote her keep and the employment of nurses for her sons; and she experienced freedom from the normal wifely obligations which might have constrained her autonomy. When Archibald returned to Sydney in 1845 it would be to find his wife firmly entrenched as a respected and well-known critic of colonial morals, and an activist in the cause of female, and family, migrants. She was well on the path to fame, not only in the colonies, but in metropolitan Britain itself. If he had qualms about the outcome of Caroline's ventures, and about the unusual nature of his marriage relationship, Caroline's undoubted eminence overrode them. But there was no evidence at all of such misgivings. He was a man to keep a promise.

As Caroline first walked about Sydney streets, the sad circumstances of many very young migrant women came before her alert scrutiny. Young women, mostly Irish, and many no more than fourteen, fifteen or sixteen years of age, had been ejected from their home lands, orphanages and workhouses supposedly to supply domestic servants in the colony. The more presentable of their peers had found favour with mistresses, but others, poor, bedraggled and friendless, slept in parks and streets, near starvation, losing hope, and vulnerable to sexual exploitation. None of the upper-class Sydney ladies who were active in charity exerted themselves on the young women's behalf, since they regarded them as disreputable, prostitutes even. Caroline interceded with some of her acquaintances to find the girls positions as servants. Other young women, obviously in need of care, and training, she took into her own home, up to ten at a time. One by one, they moved on to employers. Caroline was horrified that callous planners at both ends of the migration chain should so disregard the vulnerable situation of poverty-stricken women.

Caroline plunged determinedly into activism after Archibald's departure. Her efforts to work informally placing young women in contact with employers were clearly inadequate, as more and more

'A carol on Caroline Chisholm'

waves of women were dispatched to Sydney's shores. The sight of the degradation suffered by one young and beautiful Highland girl at the hands of a wealthy married seducer enraged her. 'From this period', Caroline wrote in her own account of her work for female immigration, published in 1842, 'I devoted all my *leisure* time in endeavouring to serve these poor girls, and felt determined, with God's blessing, never to rest until *decent protection* was afforded them'. She planned to beg the Governor, Sir George Gipps, for the use of the disused Immigration Barracks for a refuge. How would she, an unknown, female newcomer of very modest social standing, bring influence to bear upon so august a personage?

> For three weeks I hesitated, and suffered much. I was prepared to encounter the opposition of some, the lukewarmness, or the actual hostility of others, to the plan I might suggest. I saw I must have the aid of the Press; for I could only anticipate success by soliciting public sympathy for the cause I had undertaken, notwithstanding which, as a female and almost a stranger in the colony, I naturally felt diffident. I was impressed with the idea, that God had, in a peculiar manner, fitted me for this work; and yet I hesitated . . . My delay pressed on my mind as a *sin*; and when I heard of a poor girl suffering distress and losing her reputation in consequence, I felt that I was not *clear of her sin*, for I did not do all I *could* to prevent it.

On Easter Sunday, 1841, she finally decided: she must offer her talents to the God who gave them. To save these girls from sin, she would 'sacrifice my feelings—surrender all comfort—nor, in fact, consider my own wishes or feelings, but wholly devote myself to the work I had in hand. I felt my offering was accepted, and that God's blessing was on my work . . . '.[5]

One of Caroline Chisholm's biographers, Mary Hoban, contributes a further inspiration for Caroline's resolute period of activism. Caroline read a book, *The American Mother*, published in 1839, which spoke much to Caroline's way of thinking about the duties and obligations of the new wife. The writer of this prescriptive text described the example of the style of wife who was not to be emulated. This wife, once a 'gentle, amiable and affectionate daughter', turns into a 'gentle, amiable and affectionate wife'. But she had few independently held principles, and commanded little respect from her husband: 'for how much communion of soul can there be between a highly-cultivated and well-informed man, and a weak and ignorant woman?'. This wife had not taken responsibility for herself as a 'rational and immortal being' to be accountable for her own conscience before God. The writer stressed instead that a woman must take social as well as familial leadership in morals and behaviour, an exercise of influence especially important on pioneering frontiers. If others were 'silent, tongue-tied, timid, fearful' in the face of evil, the true wife, the true woman, always resolutely stood up to be counted.[6]

Caroline worked initially in two areas: protecting working-class women from sexual predators and silly young marriages by arming them with skills and waged work: and then taming the wild male sex by getting them into decent marriages with good wives. She also considered the plight of migrant married women and men with numerous young children whose poverty and material insecurity were scandalous to her eye, and whose bad treatment was symptomatic of the disordered colonial attitudes to decent gender arrangements. Caroline moved from empirical observation to generalisation and theory, attempting ultimately to shape local colonial policy on immigration and settlement in New South Wales. Her first attempt at restructuring the early experiences of single women was her decision to acquire the Immigration Barracks as a refuge and a base from which assistance in employment could be made. Her mobilisation of local support for this scheme was hampered by Protestant fears of ulterior Catholic imperialism, particularly since not only was Caroline a Roman Catholic but so were many of the Irish women in need. She slowly made an impression on many suspicious gentlemen, who came to speak of Caroline's disarming openness, honesty, frankness and genuine wish to help people of any faith. Her approach to the Governor was made decorously through a letter to Lady Gipps. Granted an audience with Gipps, Caroline faced him without embarrassment. Sir George later told a friend that he 'expected to have seen an old lady in white cap and spectacles, who would have talked to me about my soul. I was amazed when my aide introduced a handsome, stately young woman who proceeded to reason the question as if she thought her reason and experience, too, worth as much as mine'.[7] The use of the barracks was granted—and Caroline was swift to detect another woman's hand in the affair: 'In acknowledging this boon, I would thank Lady Gipps for her kind and generous support; she strewed a few flowers in my path—I knew them by their fragrance, and I thanked God she had a woman's heart'.[8]

The homeless girls and women were thankful enough to move into the barracks, judging by the numbers who sought refuge. But affairs would not go smoothly unless there was some focus and direction for the centre. Braving the unknown, Caroline moved in with her small sons.

Amidst the other difficulties of organising makeshift sleeping, eating and washing arrangements for a hundred or more women, she had to confront the rats—hundreds of them. Poison worked. Then there were the human prowlers.

> When I first opened the Home, the greater part of my duty was of a very unpleasant nature—sailors, soldiers, draymen and gentlemen would visit the home; and as there were several doors, I had no sooner turned one party out and returned to the office, than it was reported to me that another was in. I was almost weary of telling them—'These are the single women's quarters, you cannot stay here!'.[9]

Lastly, she confronted the difficulties of caring for her own children adequately on this site, with her attentions directed elsewhere much of the time. The two older boys were wanderers amidst the excitement and dangers of horses, drays, construction sites: they were despatched back home to Windsor with the housekeeper. Little Henry, at two, was easier to keep confined, and Caroline hesitated to relinquish him as well. 'Some sickness among the children in the tents told me plainly my duty, still I would not, could not give him up. A lady whose esteem I value told me I could not, must not, risk my child's life; that I must either give up the Home, or my selfish feeling for my child.' She was caught between her maternal feelings and her work for the girls who had nowhere else to go. 'On my return to the office, I found a poor woman waiting to ask for a white gown to make *her dead bairn decent*. I went into my room, packed up my little fellow's wardrobe, and the next day he was at Windsor. This was the *last sacrifice* it was God's will to *demand*.'[10] Now Archibald was in single male officers' quarters in Madras, thousands of miles away, their three sons were 8 miles distant with the company of a nurse, and Caroline was living in sparse accommodation with a hundred poor single women in the middle of Sydney. But in no way was this viewed by either of the married couple as a dereliction of social, marital or parental duty. Both were serving their Maker's cause—which they also saw as their country's cause—by allowing Caroline space for her God-given talents, while Archibald earned their living serving his country in his way, on a distant foreign frontier. Their children were early brought within the orbit of their parents' principled decisions, and, as their children, would come to share the sacrifices, as well as the joys, of family concerns.

The next challenge Caroline overcame was the migrant women's fear of the interior, the 'bush', where a demand for domestic servants could be created, if it didn't already exist. She wrote to local notables in country districts enquiring about the possibilities of work for women, of the likely conditions and wages, and the expenses the women would face purchasing their necessary goods. Offers of employment came in. Drays were borrowed to transport the women to their distant households. But the women, though desperate for work, were nervous of leaving the refuge of the city. Stories of the bush frightened them. They dreaded isolation from familiar sights. Caroline decided she must accompany them. Off she went, with successive waves of young women, into the interior. With the women she slept under the drays, or in the open air, occasionally within the haven of a friendly owner's homestead or pub. Caroline used the journeys to search out new places, and to monitor the suitability of earlier engagements. She succeeded over time in establishing a system that could operate without her personal presence, though she took great pride in matching the needs of enquirers and the domestic servant dispatched. She had a sharp eye for possible male predatoriness, and would send women only to households where another woman was present. She became aware of households where the husband was disposed to harass the servants, and took care to send to such homes only very plain young women. According to Roger Therry, 'In progress of time her name acquired quite a talismanic influence as their protectress ... Improper advances, made by masters and their servants to these girls, were successfully defeated by the bare threat to the assailant that they would write and complain to Mrs. Chisholm'.[11]

Couples with many young children were also in trouble. If the man could not sustain waged employment in Sydney, the chances of his being acceptable to rural employers was slight. Yet these families, Chisholm asserted, were the right people to settle the land: 'single men have nearly ruined this colony', she wrote to the editors of the *Sydney Morning Herald* in January 1844. 'Let me ask the advocates of the bachelor system, what have they done for the colony? Answer. Nothing! It is a source of satisfaction for me to know that I have broken up the Bachelor System ... and been enabled to introduce matrimony into the bush.'[12] Men were not good without women; women needed good men.

There was no suggestion that this applied to Archibald's and Caroline's long absence from each other, though one bachelor, at least, had looked with approving eyes at Caroline. Thomas Callaghan wrote in his diary in February 1842,

> Therry asked me to take tea with him, and I went to his home. Mrs. Chisholm came in and spent the evening there: only that she is a little too old and married I should not be unlikely to transfer to her my home affections; she seems to be a woman of more than ordinary firmness, activity and intelligence of character: I think that she has a kind heart, and I consider her as decidedly good-looking.

Married or not, he obviously could not dismiss amorous intentions. The next day he went to call on Caroline at the Home. 'She was sitting there writing hard amidst a bevy of women assembled around her in a small and crowded room: she looked very well and happy: but this must be terrible work for a lady, and it's apparently done for charity's sake. Our interview was short and satisfactory to me.' He sent a subscription, and received a kindly note in turn. On 27 February, 'coming from church, I met Mrs. Chisholm and she gave me a very friendly salute . . . and upon my return home, I wrote a long note to Mrs. Chisholm'. Caroline obviously felt some slight alarm: 'At about 10, received a note by messenger from Mrs. Chisholm explaining my misconceptions about the purport of her former note to me: it was kindly and anxiously written'.[13] And that put an end to it.

In March 1845 Caroline welcomed Archibald back from India. Archibald, at forty-seven, had retired from active service on an invalid pension which reduced his modest army pay even further. They moved into accommodation in the Queen's Head Inn in the city, planning a return trip to England. There were relations to see again after thirteen or fourteen years' absence. But Caroline mainly intended to carry her campaign about migration back to the British government. From now on, Caroline would have from Archibald a single-minded devotion to her cause in practice as well as principle. For a man to consent to his wife's life of public activism was rare enough. For him to assist her work in a quiet and self-effacing manner was indeed remarkable. But that remarkable marital relationship eventuated. Archibald, like many a colonial dignitary, was clearly under the spell of Caroline's charismatic personality, and her influence over him remained undimmed.

With Archibald's wholehearted assent, Caroline decided to bring her campaign to London. Before they left for England they undertook an unusual journey, to gather details about the style of living of the families settled on small holdings. Caroline had deliberately delayed this long-planned excursion until Archibald's return. Her work with immigrants and unemployed people, she explained, had been 'attended with certain expenses and responsibilities', and she did not feel justified in outlaying this further money 'without the sanction and approval of my husband'.[14] Archibald duly agreed, accompanied her on her trip to collect previously distributed questionnaires, and paid for the printing of the report she wrote. In it she begged British colonial officials, in particular the Secretary of State for the Colonies, Earl Grey, for migration assistance for more single women, assistance for the wives, children and aged parents left behind by Australian colonists, and for help to settle impoverished parents of large families on small farms where they could acquire a modest self-sufficiency. Urban living was not conducive to decent, moral, humane social relations, she asserted. More waged work for women might tempt girls to stay single, and encourage 'lazy and indolent men to depend more upon their wives' industry than upon their own exertions, thus partly reversing the design of nature'. Thus it would be 'until the inequality of the sexes is removed'. Farmhouses had room for cradles for babies, and armchairs for grandparents. The 'frightful disparity of the sexes' was the cause of much misery and violence, not least towards Aboriginal women: if England did not care about the happiness of her own children, 'the gradual destruction and extermination of the Aborigines DEMAND it from her justice!!!', Caroline wrote emphatically. Grey should think on all this when he found himself in some tranquil domestic moment.

> For all the clergy you can despatch, all the school-masters you can appoint, all the churches you can build, and all the books you can export, will never do much good without what a gentleman in that Colony very appropriately called 'God's police'—wives and little children—good and virtuous women.[15]

The degradation of men was desperately apparent once they were separated from domestic influences.

If the power of her pen would not move British officials, Caroline's charismatic presence would add force to her campaign. She and Archibald left for England in March 1846, their three sons with them. A fourth son, Sydney, was born on board ship on 12 August: the pregnancy and the prospect of a shipboard confinement had not deterred Caroline or Archibald from undertaking the trip.

In London the Chisholms set about finding a house, with economy of rent and convenience of location the dominant criteria, over familial considerations of gardens, clean air or space. Eventually they settled in a small house in Islington, where callers and enquirers shared living space with the family, in a growing household. Caroline's mother came to live with them, not to occupy an armchair by the fireplace, but to assist with the care of the children, a considerable task. Two more babies, daughters named Caroline and Monica, were born in 1848 and 1851 during their mother's stay in London. Caroline was 43 years old when the second daughter arrived, her last child. In addition, Caroline took into their cramped quarters clerks as assistants, and a series of young Irish orphans who were to be trained in the domestic arts, and serve as household helps in the meantime. It appeared an unlikely context for a woman to engage in a high-profile public reform campaign, but Caroline did so. The oldest sons were drafted into action, for their parents believed they should share in the responsibilities, and personal sacrifice of money and leisure, which the cause demanded. (Monica later recalled that the children even gave up food when necessary. If a stranger arrived at dinner time, he would be invited to stay, and the children each gave up a portion from their own plates.) Caroline had, however, an immensely valuable assistant, for Archibald was willing to devote himself entirely as an active lieutenant in his wife's agenda about empire, rather than, as formerly, the army's.

The central focus of the Chisholms' activities became the establishment of the Family Colonization Loan Society, as the mechanism for assisting poor people, including families with young children, to migrate to the Australian colonies. This meant persuading Colonial Office officials that this scheme was, pragmatically or morally, in the interests of Britain. It meant persuading philanthropists to donate money for loans to departing colonists, and to finance ships, crew and food for the long voyages to Australia. It meant encouraging impoverished British citizens to hope for a better life on that distant frontier, where they would till the soil, harvest a modest patrimony, and repay loans to their benefactors. To this end Caroline gave interviews to the lowly and the mighty, she undertook speaking tours across the British Isles, she answered, with Archibald's invaluable assistance, mountains of mail. (She asserted at one stage that letters 'occupied nearly the whole of [her time] and the best part of Captain Chisholm's to answer').[16] And she was successful in gaining support, and in seeing successive vessels, crammed with migrants, sail for colonial shores.

Meanwhile not only Caroline, but Archibald and the nature of their family life, came under some public scrutiny. What people saw depended very much on their own degree of commitment to the migration cause, and their own expectations of proper middle-class household arrangements. The publisher Eneas Mackenzie was one of many prominent Londoners who admired Caroline immensely. He portrayed Caroline as 'stately in her bearing, frank, easy, and lady-like in her manners; her mouth expresses the firmness and decision of her character; her eyes are grey, penetrating in their glance; and her countenance beaming with kindness, which at once causes confidence in her intentions'. He praised the married pair. 'Our admiration is due both to her and her husband, for the self-sacrificing disposition they have evinced in sacrificing all domestic comfort . . . to carry out . . . a common object.' In this, Mackenzie included their willingness to undergo a prolonged separation. Of the children Mackenzie wrote, 'It is truly gratifying to see the species of adoration and love with which they look upon their amiable parents'.[17] Another admirer, Samuel Sidney, applauded the character of Caroline's philanthropy, in that she had abandoned comfort for hard work and frugal living, and like her 'noble-hearted husband', refused financial rewards. 'Her children, from their earliest years, are enlisted in the good work.'[18] Charles Dickens, the noted author, on the other hand, visited the Chisholms and reported: 'I dream of Mrs. Chisholm and her housekeeping. The dirty faces of her children are my continual companions'.[19] Her small, crowded house, the confusion of public and private activities, the appearance of two small children amidst his interview, had not impressed him favourably, despite his inherent sympathy for dispatching impoverished citizens to the colonies. When his novel *Bleak House* appeared, there were a few who presumed that the character of the missionary-minded lady Mrs Jellyby, with her quiet cipher of a husband, her resentful, imposed-upon older children and neglected younger children, was in part derived from his glimpse of the Chisholm ménage. For most contemporaries, there was no fit. The majority accepted Mackenzie's estimate, that 'Piety, in deeds as well as words, matrimonial, filial and paternal love knit together and form one of the happiest family circles'.[20] Caroline's and Archibald's interpretation of 'home', after all, was 'not merely a place of shelter but a place where the door might be open for everybody'.[21]

Caroline and Archibald sustained another three-year separation from 1851 to 1854 so that Archibald could act as an agent for the Family Colonization Loan Society out in the colonies, organising its affairs and collecting repayments on migrants' loans. 'We determined to work thus', Caroline wrote; 'my husband saw that it was necessary that some one devoted to the work should proceed to the colonies'. She called attention to 'a golden chain of domestic feeling, which is bridging the seas between England and Australia'.[22] In a letter to the *Daily News* she warned, however, that with their means, it would not be possible that the separation could continue for any great length of time. Archibald acquitted himself, as usual, in exemplary fashion, refusing any payment. 'I wish therefore (and I know I can speak for Mrs. Chisholm as well as for myself)', he wrote from Melbourne, 'that as far as we are concerned our Labours in this respect should end in the same spirit in which it began':[23] that is, in an honorary capacity. The society in turn recorded their deep sense of gratitude for the 'unwearied exertions' of Captain Chisholm.

Caroline and the children were reunited with Archibald in Melbourne in July 1854. Archibald having now reached the official retiring age, the army promoted him, as a courtesy extended to retiring officers, to the rank of major. And 'Major Chisholm' he became, with Caroline herself referring to him, at home and abroad, as 'The Major'. To supplement his retirement pay, Archibald and the oldest sons opened a store at Kyneton, hoping to profit from the burgeoning trade created by the gold rushes. Caroline now turned her attention to that other side of the gold diggings, the behaviour of men in groups, wife desertion, and the poor conditions for mothers of young children travelling to the goldfields. 'A new and energetic spirit is at work amongst us now . . .', declared the *Bendigo Advertiser*; 'the great and good Mrs. Chisholm is applying the energies of her masculine mind to the subject of social reform among the people of the diggings'.[24] But the store failed to prosper, and ill health beset Caroline, kidney trouble aggravated by an accident. In 1858 the pair moved to Sydney in search of a better climate. Archibald became a draper's assistant, while Caroline tried in turn decorative work for confectioners, teaching English to Chinese men, and setting up a small private school for girls. 'I make an endeavour at this late hour to do something for myself and my two little girls', she explained.[25] She appeared in public occasionally to give public lectures, in favour of free selection, in support of early closing for shops, in support of women who bore illegitimate children as a result of male seduction. She defended herself defiantly against criticism. 'Some people seemed to speak as if they thought that no woman ought to have any opinions'.[26]

She thus acknowledged some singularity in her conduct, just as years before, when she wrote her account of the founding of the Female Immigrants' Home, she saw herself as the first woman author in the colonies. But slowly there seemed less need of, or at least less response to, the Chisholms and their campaigns. The couple left Sydney for London in 1866, where they lived in obscurity and relative penury until 1877. In March that year Caroline died, after being for years a bedridden invalid. Archibald was too ill to attend her funeral, and died himself five months later, in August 1877. Caroline was sixty-eight years of age, Archibald eighty-one years. They were buried in the same grave in the cemetery at Northampton, the place of their marriage almost forty-seven years before.

Their marriage had proved an eventful one. Caroline had achieved fame, while Archibald had for forty-seven long years sustained his promise to support her philanthropic ventures. Indeed, their daughter Monica was to write of her father as a man 'of noble, self-sacrificing instincts, and much of the success of my mother's work is due to him, who, at any cost to his own comfort, was ever ready to help'.[27] Of few other Victorian husbands could this have been said. In a letter written some years before to Robert Lowe, Caroline had observed: 'I often think that there are more matched than mated, but you and Mrs. Lowe are like my dear husband and myself; you have but one mind between you'.[28] There had certainly been a remarkable coincidence of their gendered attachment to the empire, as soldier and reformer, and of their personal gifts as husband and wife. It was a remarkable Victorian marriage, mutually loving, and for Caroline, empowering.

The damned whore and the public man: Sarah and William Wentworth

Carol Liston

William Charles Wentworth is among the best known Australian historical figures, celebrated as Australia's first native-born lawyer and one of the party who crossed the Blue Mountains in 1813. He established the first independent newspaper, led the campaign to give political rights to former convicts, demanded political independence from Britain, drafted the Constitution, proposed a hereditary colonial aristocracy and was one of the founders of the University of Sydney. Visitors have admired his Sydney home, 'Vaucluse House', since the government acquired it in 1911. But a house is also a home, a physical manifestation of the lives of parents, children, relations and servants who lived there.

Visitors to Vaucluse House, entering now from the west, see the imposing grandeur of the stone-flagged verandah, the turreted roof line and curtained french windows. A visitor in the mid-nineteenth century would have approached the house along a carriage road on the opposite, eastern side. Entering through a simple garden gate, the visitor was immediately in the heart of a large working household. The covered walkway across the stone-flagged courtyard linked the residence to the kitchen wing, housekeeper's office, schoolroom and Wentworth's office. Turning right into the house, the visitor entered a long black-and-white marble-floored corridor from which doorways and staircases led to sitting rooms and domestic apartments. Visitors on business rather than social calls turned left in the courtyard to the offices.

This abrupt entrance into the heart of the household was a stark contrast to the formal, imposing entrance halls of other great colonial houses such as 'Elizabeth Bay House' or 'Lyndhurst', or even the simpler residences of 'Elizabeth Farm' at Parramatta or St Mathew's Rectory at Windsor. In these houses, visitors waited in the entrance hall while the household determined the appropriate response to the visit—to accept a social call or to conduct a business arrangement. The difference at Vaucluse House reflected social rather than financial influences on the architecture. The absence of a grand entrance is tangible evidence of the nature of the marriage of William and Sarah Wentworth, a marriage which spanned decades of major social changes in New South Wales. A convict settlement became a free colony and the wealth generated by wool and gold laid new relationships over older social patterns forged in the convict years. Public perceptions of William and Sarah's relationship were coloured by those changes.

William Charles Wentworth married Sarah Cox at St James' Church, Sydney, in October 1829. Witnesses to the ceremony were his friend and political associate, Robert Campbell junior and Sarah's sister, Elizabeth Todhunter. It was a marriage that must have titillated the gossips of Sydney, for Wentworth, wild but wealthy, had chosen to marry his mistress.

Marriages in the early years of colonial New South Wales were not as frequent as the authorities desired. Many convicts (and their military and naval guards) had left spouses behind in Britain. Relationships were formed without benefit of the clergy's blessing. Clergy were few and performed more bigamous marriages than they cared to admit. Both William Wentworth and Sarah Cox were children of unions not sanctified by the church. Their family backgrounds were common enough in convict New South Wales.

William Wentworth, son of colonial surgeon and highwayman D'Arcy Wentworth, was born on a convict ship on its way to Norfolk Island in 1790. His convict mother, Catherine Crowley, lived with D'Arcy Wentworth and bore him three sons before her death in 1800. Three years later her eldest son was sent to England to be educated under the immediate care of Wentworth's agent and under the notice of his father's relative and patron, Earl Fitzwilliam. At the end of William's schooling, he returned to New South Wales, dabbled in pastoral and commercial activities, joined the expedition over the

Blue Mountains, created a political furore and departed for England in 1816 to study law. His political awareness had been raised but seemingly not his social sensitivity. He remained unaware of his father's ambiguous social position, caused by D'Arcy's trials for highway robbery in 1787, until it was brutally brought to his attention by comments in the House of Commons in 1819. William's return to New South Wales in 1810 also coincided with the birth of a half-brother, the first child of his father's relationship with a free woman, Ann Lawes McNeal, who left her husband and child to live with D'Arcy Wentworth. She and Wentworth had a large family and Ann was pregnant with their eighth child when D'Arcy died in 1827.

At the age of thirty-five, in August 1824, William Charles Wentworth returned to New South Wales with much fanfare, clutching a law degree and ambitious to make a name for himself as a radical young man. He had published a best-selling book about Australia and owned a newspaper printing press. He established a legal practice in his lodgings in Macquarie Place, not far from the blacksmith's shop owned by Francis Cox. Cox was the father of four daughters and over the next few months Wentworth established a relationship with Sarah, Cox's eldest daughter, a 20-year-old milliner's apprentice. By March 1825 they were lovers.

Sarah Cox was the daughter of emancipists. Her father had left a wife and family in England when he was transported in 1790, so her parents never married, though her mother Fanny Morton was commonly known as Mrs Cox. A convict transported for life, Fanny had arrived in Sydney in 1796 and four years later bore her first child to Francis Cox. Sarah was born in 1805 and three sisters followed. Her father was not as prosperous as his emancipist neighbours Simeon Lord and Mary Reibey, but his blacksmithy specialising in maritime work operated successfully for nearly three decades. The relationship between Francis Cox and Fanny Morton was a stable one that survived reunions with Cox's English-born children and endured until Cox's death in 1831.

Wentworth's sexual dalliance with Sarah Cox was probably not intended to be more than a short-lived affair. It seems likely that this was Sarah's first sexual relationship. Her former fiancée, John Payne, a ship's captain, had not spent much time in Sydney and Sarah described herself during her engagement as a good and respectable girl, denying implications that she was promiscuous. In May 1825 Sarah prosecuted Payne for breach of promise to marry her when he rejected her affections for those of a wealthy emancipist widow. Sarah's prosecution created a legal sensation as it was the first case of its kind in the colony. She won £100 for the damage her reputation had suffered from the broken engagement.

Though it is easy to interpret Sarah's action against her fiancée as that of a woman defending her honour, the evidence is more ambiguous. Undoubtedly Wentworth, who was Sarah's lawyer, had persuaded her to take action against Payne. Furthermore, the evidence throws a disturbing light on Sarah's relationship with William. Propinquity alone may not have been the origin of William's attraction to Sarah. He was assembling evidence for various commercial cases involving Payne and his associates. At best he may have wanted to learn more of his opponent from Sarah; at worst, Wentworth may have deliberately engineered his relationship with Sarah to discover grounds on which he could embarrass her former fiancée.[1]

On Sarah's part, it would have been hard to reject the advances of the native-born man of the hour, despite his well-known drunken, swearing boisterous habits, habits which offended the elite free groups but attracted less condemnation from the emancipist tradesmen and shopkeepers with whom the Cox family associated.

When Sarah became pregnant, Wentworth moved her from Sydney to the privacy of a rented estate at Petersham. Their daughter, Thomasine, was born there in December 1825 and baptised in Sydney the following month as the child of Sarah Cox and W. C. Wentworth of Petersham. Sarah lived there as his mistress until 1827, when Wentworth purchased the Vaucluse estate and she, pregnant again, moved to the cottage overlooking the harbour. The move to Vaucluse coincided with an unsettled period in Wentworth's life. His father died unexpectedly, leaving a considerable fortune. Sudden wealth—and sudden insecurity—produced reckless and offensive behaviour, drunken arrogance and political ineptitude and gave much ammunition for his critics, who described him as 'an infamous Blackguard, and in every respect worthy of his birth, his being the Son of an Irish Highwayman by a Convict Whore'.[2] Sarah also seemed distant from him. Their son was born in December 1827 but when she took the baby to be baptised in January she named him William Charles but recorded that the father was unknown.

Two years later, Sarah and her children were still living under Wentworth's protection at Vaucluse and she was pregnant again. A poem appeared in the *Australian*, signed 'W. C.' and addressed to Sarah.

> For I must love thee, love thee on,
> 'Till life's remotest latest minute;
> And when the light of life is gone,—
> Thou'lt find its *lamp*—had *thee* within it.[3]

A proposal? A month later they married. Marriage had been an unlikely element in their relationship. It is difficult to believe that their initial liaison was intended to be of long standing. Two pregnancies had provided more permanent and tangible evidence of their relationship but did not demand marriage. Their parents had enjoyed long and stable relationships without the legal formality of marriage. Sarah could have been cast off for a new mistress with no stigma attached to Wentworth, provided that he made some arrangement for the children's support. Equally, Sarah could have married someone other than the father of her children.

Certainly a wealthy, educated man in Wentworth's position could have looked for a more advantageous match than marriage to the blacksmith's daughter, though the coarse behaviour so often disparaged by his contemporaries may have made Wentworth an unpalatable son-in-law for many families. He had, a decade earlier, aimed as high as a dynastic alliance through marriage to one of the daughters of John Macarthur, but Macarthur had rejected his approach. Fondness for his children and love for Sarah may have finally prompted Wentworth to regularise his domestic arrangements. Without the aura of his father's presence, Wentworth may have felt the need to put down his own roots and create a place where he belonged. Love, or perhaps a need to be loved, seems to have overcome social and economic differences.

But men cannot marry their mistresses and expect their wives to be accepted by high society. Marriage for Sarah was the start, not the end, of her social problems. Nor was William faithful to her. Within three months of their wedding, he had a brief affair with the wife of one of his political colleagues. The paternity of the child that resulted from this liaison was probably common knowledge. It was publicly acknowledged when the boy was baptised a decade later and W. C. Wentworth was named as the father. Wentworth's opponents referred to him as a 'self-confessed adulterer'.[4] Possibly there were other infidelities, though Wentworth's popularity as a political figure in these years suggests that children were named in his honour without necessarily implying paternity.

Sarah's background as Wentworth's mistress effectively restricted her social life to her own family circle. Barely literate, her few letters and her portraits present her as a calm, determined and practical woman. Whatever her knowledge of Wentworth's infidelities in the early 1830s, she referred to him at that time as her 'kind husband'. These years, with Wentworth busy with his legal practice and politics and Sarah constantly ill with miscarriages, were probably difficult ones. The second part of the decade saw a stabilising of their relationship, when William retired from the Bar and they moved

Sarah Wentworth in the 1860s

semi-permanently to their country estate, 'Windermere', in the Hunter Valley to supervise his expanding pastoral empire. Here, away from the political and social pressures of Sydney, close to Sarah's sister and her family, life could establish a more natural rhythm.[5] These years in the late 1830s saw a deepening of the relationship between Sarah and William. His temper, always on a short fuse in the years that he practised at the Bar, improved. In 1840 William turned fifty; Sarah was thirty-five.

Sarah and William Wentworth had ten children—two born prior to their marriage, the third a few weeks after their wedding, then a gap of four years until the birth of Fitzwilliam in 1833. Babies then followed at regular two- to three-year intervals. A stillborn child in 1850 marked the end of twenty-five years' fertility. The social isolation of Vaucluse and Windermere probably contributed to the fact that Sarah lost none of her children to illness. Wentworth, a doctor's son, was fanatically concerned about rapid access to medical assistance for his wife and children. Their social circle was the large extended family of Wentworth's half-brothers and sisters and Sarah's parents, sisters, nephews and nieces. The Cox family in England and various Wentworth cousins also formed part of this network. Various members lived intermittently with William and Sarah at Vaucluse and Windermere. The moral failings of any of the relatives, such as Wentworth's young half-brother John, were used as warnings to improve the behaviour of their children.

Despite prosperity and her husband's political success, Sarah could not escape her past:

> as the wife's functions increased and she undertook the moral guidance and elementary education of the children it was seen as essential that she conform to bourgeois moral standards. So, although a woman characterised as a Damned Whore could marry and raise children, the stigma of the stereotype would brand her forever, in the eyes of society if not her husband, and her fitness for performing these functions would always be called into question.[6]

Sarah's humble and convict parentage could be overlooked; her sexual immorality could not. She was, forever, the damned whore. Moral failings in her family—from her husband to her grandchildren—were attributed to her poor example.

Family and the home were the private world of nineteenth-century women. It was an existence that Sarah Wentworth shared with her contemporaries; but her world was more artificially confined because of her background. She did not have the education to teach her own daughters. Her children were educated at Sydney day schools, occasionally attending as boarders when their parents were not in Sydney.

Sydney society never forgot that Sarah had been Wentworth's mistress before she was his wife. This excluded her from both public and private occasions as a political hostess. She could not help Wentworth with his public career. Neither could he defend her reputation, but stood by silently while disparaging comments were made about her morality. The significance of this social exclusion increased as their children grew older. Seven Wentworth daughters would eventually want to enjoy the same social activities as other young women of wealth and position. Seven daughters required suitable husbands. Sarah Wentworth was unable to chaperone her daughters because she was not invited to the principal social events in the colony. Excluded from the more formal social circuit of Sydney, Sarah and her daughters may have enjoyed more relaxed relationships within their family network, but ultimately social reality intruded.

Government House was the focus of colonial social life. Eliza Darling, wife of the Governor when Sarah and William married, clearly rejected her:

> It was thought that people ought to be born and educated as gentlefolks, before they should be admitted to Government House—Mr Wentworth himself as a Barrister, educated at Oxford, might certainly have been asked, but his Wife, having lived with him for years, has only recently become his wife, and when we left, used to sit at a Stall selling Beef in consequence of the very low price of Cattle and Mr Wentworth having so many Thousands he had set up a butcher shop.[7]

The visit of Governor Bourke to Vaucluse in February 1836 was enough to provoke gossip that the Governor may have met Sarah. Wentworth published a statement that the Governor had merely inspected the building works in progress and had not dined at Vaucluse, an occasion that would have required some formal contact with his hostess. Sarah's position was succinctly stated by Lady Jane Franklin—'very handsome, lady like and amiable, but of course not visited'.[8]

Sarah's dilemma was how to present her daughters to the polite world, as befitted the children of one of the colony's wealthiest and most influential men. Her problem was solved temporarily by her warm-hearted and generous sister-in-law, Eliza McPherson Wentworth, wife of Major D'Arcy Wentworth. A childless couple, when they lived in Sydney in the early 1840s Eliza and D'Arcy Wentworth squired Sarah's two older girls to social events, including musical evenings at Government House with Lady Gipps.

The 1840s was a decade of public achievement for Wentworth. Despite his positive relationship with Governor Bourke, he had been excluded from the nominated Legislative Councils of the 1830s. With a partially elected Legislative Council from 1843, Wentworth for the first time participated formally in the colony's political institutions. His stature as the leader of the non-government party meant that he was constantly in the public eye. He was at the height of his wealth and influence, yet two social incidents indicate the enormous gulf between the public and private experience—the marriage of his eldest daughter and the first colonial ball hosted by Governor FitzRoy.

In 1844 Wentworth's eldest child, Thomasine, married Thomas John Fisher, solicitor and nephew of Wentworth's friend and colleague, the late Robert Wardell. On the surface, therefore, it seemed a further link in an already established connection between two legal families. Appearances were deceptive. Fisher had come to Australia because of delays by Wentworth in settling his uncle's estate. He remained to practise law but alternated between awe for Wentworth's political and financial standing and fear that friendship with Wentworth would alienate other colonists. He declined to join the Wentworth family for a meal at Vaucluse. But Fisher's reluctance to mix socially with the family was put down to fear that he might be expected to meet Ann Lawes, D'Arcy Wentworth's mistress, or Sarah's mother, Fanny Cox, who lived at Vaucluse House. Fisher was deeply attracted to Thomasine Wentworth and in January 1844 the couple married. Wentworth gave his daughter land at Vaucluse, in Macquarie Street and at Bathurst for her marriage portion.

No sooner had the marriage vows been uttered than Fisher forbade his young wife any social contact with her parents, a ban that he maintained for twenty years. Wanting Thomasine but fearing the scorn of his friends if he mixed with the Wentworth family, he had decided to have the girl but separate her from her family. It was a cruel blow, aimed not at the older generation but at Thomasine's mother, Sarah.

Eliza Wentworth tried to mediate on Sarah's behalf. In so doing she spelt out her own views about marriage and the relationship between man and wife.

> God knows! No one has a higher idea of the duty a wife owes to her husband . . . and when his commands are lawful and just and cheerfully and most willingly should I obey them but when his commands infringe and are in direct opposition to those of my heavenly Father I would then most certainly . . . follow the dictates of my own conscience—I cannot comprehend how a husband—a Christian husband could ask his wife to forsake her parents—parents too who have ever evinced the warmest, the most devoted affection for their child.[9]

Thomasine's interpretation of her duty as wife rather than child was evident from her reaction to this ban. A 'mere child in her manners' though a 'girl of some strength of mind and intellect', she obeyed her husband's edict to avoid public—and private—meetings with her family. Only dire financial and emotional pressure after twenty years caused her to break this injunction.[10]

Wentworth coped with the estrangement from his eldest child with a disdainful and defiant attitude, confident that Fisher would relent and give in. In the meantime 'we do not consider it worth our while to court the little gentleman's acquaintance'.[11] Sarah, ever practical and perhaps aware that she was considered to blame for the situation, reminded her daughter to send home the washing and mending if she could not cope with domestic chores.[12] Colonial society was presumably aware of this tension within the Wentworth family. The family crisis coincided with the turbulent political crisis between the squatters, led by Wentworth, and Governor Gipps. This social disaster was not repeated with the marriage of their second daughter, Fanny, whose husband belonged to her parent's generation and was a business associate of her father's and already an established Victorian squatter. He did not live in Sydney so did not need to court local prejudices.

The most prestigious event on the viceregal calendar was the celebration of the monarch's birthday. Governor Gipps had been replaced by Sir Charles FitzRoy in 1846 and his first Queen's Birthday Ball was to take place in May 1847. Invitations were sent out but the ball had to be postponed when FitzRoy's son broke his leg. This allowed time for discussion of the guest list, not only in private but in the very public columns of the Sydney press. Concern

William Charles Wentworth in the 1880s

was expressed that the Governor and his wife had included people of 'doubtful reputation' among those invited to the ball. Among those whose attendance was considered unsuitable was Sarah Wentworth. Elizabeth Macarthur, who had never met Sarah, wrote that

> the Chief Justice has ventured to object to some persons invited to Govt House—I believe there are two others that find fault but have not given publicity to their opinions—the Ladies have taken umbrage by the introduction of Mrs Wentworth and one or two others.[13]

For Sarah, with her two older daughters married and her sister-in-law living in Van Diemen's Land, the possibility of establishing herself socially with the new governor was an important opportunity for her to fulfil her role as social chaperone for her younger daughters. Her husband's political pre-eminence meant that the Wentworths qualified, in terms of public position, to attend viceregal functions. But Sarah's invitation became the catalyst for public debate in a community self-consciously aware that its convict origins cast doubts over the moral integrity of the whole colony, but especially of its women.

The occasion, in all its cruel absurdity, was summarised by Colonel Mundy. Among the 1200 occasional visitors to Government House, umbrage was taken at the inclusion of 'two or three persons far advanced in years and much esteemed by those who knew them, who in the somewhat lax infancy of the colony had . . . taken on themselves parental responsibilities without due regard to ritual'.[14] Because of their noble rank by birth, both FitzRoy and his wife could mix with the lowly and the immoral without fear that their reputations would be tarnished. Colonists were more circumspect. One's character was determined by the status of the people with whom one mixed. The press, whether as creators or followers of public opinion, demanded that viceregal functions be uncontaminated by the presence of immoral women so that the wives and daughters of the elite could mingle in safety.

The *Sydney Morning Herald*, echoing the stand of its rival, the *Atlas*, demanded that the company at Government House be of the same standard as that permitted in respectable homes:

> Damaged female characters . . . albeit they had been completely and clerically repaired, should be uncompromisingly shut out . . . Whenever a woman falls, she falls for ever . . . She becomes as it were socially dead. Her punishment is indeed worse than death . . . A few individual instances of hardship may occur but a much greater number are prevented . . . There should be no statute of limitation enacted for the relief of female error. Should the reader have a wife or sister, he would not desire that she should be at any time introduced to a reformed lady of easy virtue, however romantic, peculiar or pitiable her individual case.[15]

Nevertheless, the press acknowledged that these women had been 'exemplary mothers for twenty years'. In the best English fashion, they were 'adornments to their domestic hearths', having raised well-educated sons and daughters who had married into families of rank and fortune. Eventually common sense prevailed as the debate wore itself out when it threatened to reproach too many mothers and grandmothers of respectable colonists.

The attack was specifically aimed at three women, two of whom were undoubtedly guilty of immoral conduct (Sarah Wentworth and probably Harriet Scott, newly-wed wife but previously the mistress of A. W. Scott, an eminent Hunter Valley settler) and one merely suspected of improper behaviour (possibly a sister of leading barrister Edward Broadhurst). Only Sarah Wentworth was clearly identified by her contemporaries. This attack on private behaviour was aimed at the leaders of colonial public life. It signalled a community reaction that domestic circumstances tolerated in the past would be tolerated no longer. Private lives would henceforth be an element in determining public status.

Wentworth, despite his considerable oratorical skills and political connections, was helpless against attacks like this on Sarah. He could not defend her without making the situation worse as she had not been named in the newspapers but was merely identified in private correspondence and gossip. The vicious attack of 1847 convinced Sarah that it would not be possible to bring up her younger daughters in New South Wales. They would forever carry the stigma of her actions. Though pregnancy, financial problems and political activities delayed matters, from 1847 the Wentworths rationalised their holdings and planned their move to Britain, a move which came when Fitzwilliam matriculated to university in 1852.

One of the hardest emotional burdens for colonial families was the long separation between parents and child when the children were sent away to school in England. Willie, the Wentworths' eldest son, was sent to England in 1844 at the age of seventeen. The pressures on Willie and Fitzwilliam Wentworth were increased by their father's ambition for them to succeed in law, despite the physical limitations caused by Willie's hearing and sight problems and Fitzwilliam's chronic ill health. Sarah was separated from Willie for nine years, during which time she worried constantly about his physical and emotional well-being.

Knowledge of their parents' scandalous background was kept from the younger Wentworth children but the attacks on Sarah in the 1840s could not be kept secret from the older ones. This was brought home most cruelly to Willie, who was at university in England in the 1840s. Newspaper accounts and private letters were thrust at him, proof of his mother's sin. Sarah's half-brother, John Cox, confirmed the truth of the allegations and Willie probably had a nervous breakdown. Sarah never forgave herself for leaving Willie on his own in England during this emotionally stressful time. For Willie, his illegitimacy had financial implications. Sarah's omission of his father's name on his baptismal registration meant that he was excluded from inheriting under the will of his grandfather, D'Arcy Wentworth. In legal documents in the 1850s Sarah attempted to compensate Willie for this loss by allocating to him her dower entitlements, established as trust funds on her behalf by Wentworth during the uncertain economic conditions of the 1840s. Sarah made the usual provisions for her daughters and grandchildren but the bequests were structured to provide an income for life for her eldest, but illegitimate and disinherited son.[16]

When Fitzwilliam matriculated, Sarah was determined not to let him go to England alone, but personal and public duties had conflicting timetables. Wentworth's political commitment to the separation of the colony from British control and the drafting of a constitution establishing responsible government required his presence in the colony for a further year. Wentworth urged Sarah to take the children and go without him. Initially she resisted, but uncertainty about Willie overcame her reluctance and in February 1853 she sailed for England with her 20-year-old son, the six youngest children and a companion governess, leaving her husband behind.

Wentworth joined her in London in June 1854. This fifteen months was the longest separation of their marriage and Sarah felt unsettled until they were reunited.[17] Her acceptance in London as the wife of a wealthy colonist and prominent statesman gave her and her daughters greater freedom than they had ever enjoyed in the colony. London was a 'place where women are treated better than any other place . . . for they are loved and cared for here'.[18]

Both referred to their stay in Britain as an exile, made necessary by the need to educate their children and see the Constitution Bill through the British Parliament. Half tempted to take up public life in Britain, but not wanting to commit himself to a permanent home there, Wentworth involved himself with colonial lobby groups. Now in his mid-sixties, there was little prospect of a colonial political career if he returned to the newly responsible legislature. One outcome of the Wentworth family's move to Europe was that Sarah was able to entertain her husband's associates. Far from the gossips of Sydney, Sarah Wentworth in Paris and London entertained a cross-section of colonial expatriates and European business associates.

Her daughters' educations were Sarah's predominant concern and 'on this point she is inexorable. She says we came home to educate the girls and that they cannot be properly educated in the country which is probably true enough', commented her husband in explanation of his failure to take up the life of a country gentleman.[19] In rented houses in London, Belgium, Paris and a number of fashionable European resorts, the Wentworth girls attended schools, had governesses and mixed with other wealthy young ladies in English and European society. Sarah, conscious of her own youthful indiscretion, guarded her younger daughters carefully, considering that her 18-year-old daughter and namesake was too naive to be trusted away from her parents, even when chaperoned by Fanny, her elder married sister, whom Sarah thought also lacked worldly experience.[20]

Yet the years abroad were not happy ones. Sixteen-year-old Isabelle died in 1856; her older sister Sarah (Joody) died in Corfu the following year. Their brother Fitzwilliam was chronically ill throughout 1856 and 1857 and in 1858 Sarah found herself nursing her eldest son, Willie. He died in March 1859.

Sarah and William returned to Sydney with their four youngest children in April 1861. Their stay was a brief one but coincided with a constitutional crisis that enabled Wentworth to become active again in political life as Speaker of the Legislative Council. Sarah faced colonial public life with greater confidence than she had a decade earlier. In September 1861 she could boast to her eldest daughter that 'all the nice families . . . call on us'. Colonial society had changed and Sarah felt that, on the surface at least, it was less malicious than it had been.[21] In September 1862 William and Sarah Wentworth hosted a ball, the only occasion on which they publicly entertained colonial society—a far cry from the oft-quoted drunken entertainment Wentworth had given in the grounds of Vaucluse House on the departure of Governor Darling in 1831. Vaucluse House was, for Sarah, a private place and she did not hold the ball there, hiring instead a more convenient grand house on Woolloomooloo Hill. The Governor and his wife attended, as did the members of the Legislative Council and Assembly and many of the 'first people' in the colony. There were no reports about the damned whore this time. A month later, Sarah and William sailed for England to enrol their youngest son, D'Arcy, in school. Neither saw Australia

Vaucluse in the late 1870s

again. William Charles Wentworth died in England in 1872 and Sarah in July 1880.

Only a few letters written by William Wentworth to his wife survive; there are none written by Sarah to William. The record of their lives together lies in the comments they made to their children and friends, hardly a satisfactory basis on which to judge their marriage.

Was the marriage of Sarah and William Wentworth a successful partnership? It was not obviously so when viewed from the perspective of Wentworth's public career. Nor was the Wentworth marriage a partnership of minds or intellect. It was, perhaps, a more subtle balance of opposites.

Sarah's background as Wentworth's mistress meant that she was never accepted in the public role of the politician's wife, entertaining and cultivating political supporters. She was barely literate and though aware of her husband's projects, especially for education, was not particularly conversant with his political interests. Perhaps if her personality had been different, if she had been more aggressive and assertive, she might have pushed her way into the circles of political hostesses, but Sarah Wentworth appears not to have tried. James Macarthur, whose political relationship with Wentworth mutated from enemy to ally, met Sarah Wentworth for the first time in 1852. He found her to be a 'nice looking' woman, 'much more the Lady in manner and appearance than many who give themselves great airs of exclusiveness'.[22]

Macarthur's comment suggests that Sarah was the perfect counterpoint to the powerful persona of Wentworth. Tall and athletic in build, Wentworth was considered even by his political enemies to be intellectually, as well as physically, head and shoulders above his contemporaries. More often criticised than praised in the lively political interchanges of the 1840s and early 1850s, he was described as a 'commanding ruin' of a man, slovenly and disrespectful in bearing, his harsh drawl a discordant sound to those who heard him speak, his florid countenance evidence of hard living.[23] His public accomplishments in the political arena were not offset, in Wentworth's opinion, by 'the rabid abuse to which every act of my public life for years past has been subjected'.[24] The criticism of his private life added another overlooked dimension to this abuse, and left him unusually powerless, even contrite.

Nor could Sarah contribute wealth or social prestige to their marriage. Yet despite the outward disparity in their situations, Sarah provided essential resources for Wentworth's business and pastoral interests. His brother and half-brothers had the means to develop their own financial interests, but Sarah's relations were looking for opportunity as much as Wentworth needed trustworthy assistants. Her brothers-in-law and nephews found employment in the expanding Wentworth empire, managing his urban and rural properties from the mid-1820s until Wentworth's death.

Sarah's father was not a wealthy man, but on his death in 1831 he was able to leave two portions of land in Sydney to his daughters. Sarah inherited a half-share in the site of his blacksmith's shop, Cox's Wharf at Circular Quay. The property was rented out and she received the rents. One indication of her independence of mind was her management of this income. She felt strongly that it was hers to use as she chose. When her sister sent the rent money to Wentworth, Sarah was annoyed, exclaiming that she did not 'object to his receiving it but I have the right to have it paid to whom I wish'.[25] Sarah's management skills were the product of years of dealing with a family of ten children and a household of servants. She took pride in the mundane housekeeping skill of compiling inventories, a task she frequently found herself undertaking alone as her family moved between lodgings in Europe and England. She criticised her sister's inability to provide a correct inventory. As Wentworth's health

Entrance Hall, Vaucluse House, 1869: portrait busts including those of Sarah Wentworth and her daughter Thomasine (Charles Abrahams, *c.* 1844) dominate the hall. (Pencil sketch by Rebecca Martens)

deteriorated in the late 1860s, Sarah increasingly took over the management of their affairs. Wentworth was a notoriously poor administrator, often failing to register legal documents, and Sarah introduced more methodical arrangements so that she could keep him informed of their varied pastoral and investment projects.[26]

Marriage is ordained for the procreation of children and their appropriate up-bringing. The Wentworth marriage was fruitful. Of the ten children born to Sarah and William, seven survived their parents. By Sarah's death in 1880, eighteen grandchildren had been baptised, though four had died in early infancy. A harder question is whether the marriage of the parents provided a model for the family life of the children. Despite years of irreproachable respectability, moral failings within the family were often unfairly laid at Sarah's door.

Thomasine Fisher (1825–1913) and Fanny Reeve (1829–93) married early and had satisfactory, stable relationships with their husbands. Thomasine learnt by accident of her grandfather Cox's convict past as late as 1866. The two older girls, respectably married, recognised that their own morality would always be suspect because of their mother. Their response was to turn to religion and good works—and to live in Britain. Thomasine, concerned about her younger sisters and the effect of her father's outspoken secularism, urged her mother to ensure the girls had religious instruction. Sarah rather tartly commented that she should give Wentworth more credit for his concern for his children. Despite his own scepticism, Wentworth recognised that religious conformity was an essential element for his daughters' respectability. In old age he became the principal target of their missionary efforts.[27]

Sarah had arranged for her grandson, Willie Fisher, to work on one of the Wentworth pastoral stations. He took an Aboriginal girl as his mistress and when they were separated by the station manager, he committed suicide in May 1868. Sarah blamed herself for not taking greater care of him, having been deterred because she did not want the managers to think that he was 'Old Wentworth's spy' and receiving special treatment. The colonial press made much of the rumours that surrounded Willie's death and the subsequent death of the station manager.[28]

Fitzwilliam (1833–1915) married against his parent's wishes in Sydney in 1868. His bride, Mary Jane Hill, was a niece by marriage of Sarah's sister Henrietta. Their descendants form the main branch of the Wentworth family in the late twentieth century. Eliza (Didy) (1838–98) never married. The remaining three married impulsively and tragically within a month of their father's death in 1872.

D'Arcy's marriage to Lucy Bowman was already arranged and proceeded despite the funeral, though it was never consummated. They separated on the honeymoon, with Lucy blamed for the breakdown of a relationship that seemingly from the beginning had been confused by D'Arcy, who regarded her as yet another older sister. Lucy blamed Sarah for having 'done her utmost to ruin him from his childhood'. Lucy and D'Arcy led separate lives until their deaths in the 1920s. Belatedly, in 1890, D'Arcy accepted the responsibility of raising his twin daughters by an Irish girl, Anne Reilly.[29]

Two days before D'Arcy's wedding in October 1872, Edith married a 'silly little High Church curate', the Reverend Charles Dunbar, thus inheriting £25 000 under her father's will. Her fortune was soon spent repairing his churches. In 1878 Edith applied for a judicial separation and attempted, unsuccessfully, to recover her fortune and her daughter. In December 1872 Laura decided to marry Captain Henry Keays-Young rather than return with her mother to Sydney for her father's state funeral. Laura's marriage fell apart within a few years, victim of her ill health, the deaths of her daughters as infants and her husband's drinking and constant physical and mental abuse of her. Her death on her forty-fifth birthday in 1887 was, in the eyes of her brothers and sisters, a merciful release.[30]

Colonial Australia was ambivalent about Wentworth—and Wentworth and his family knew it. A public holiday was declared to mark his return to Sydney from England in 1861 and another declared for his funeral in 1872, yet the Legislative Assembly had opposed the hanging of his portrait in the Chamber in 1857 and the University of Sydney erected his statue in the Great Hall in 1862 only on condition that Wentworth did not attend the ceremony. Even while planning Wentworth's burial, Sarah and her daughters dismissed their preference for a tomb in St Andrew's Cathedral, its recumbent figure to be an echo of the Wentworth ancestral tombs in York Minster. They felt that people in Sydney would reject such a public monument.

Sarah recognised her husband's weaknesses and saw the same characteristics in their children. She thought Wentworth easily inspired and 'so very truthful that he was so often deceived like a child'. She likened her strong-willed husband and children to servants who despite constant arguing and harassment could not be forced to act. Nothing could be accomplished except by gentle guidance in the right direction. With Wentworth's death, 'the one that made our house so very cheerful' had gone.[31]

The tragedy of the Wentworth marriage was their enforced separation from their homeland. Neither wanted to be expatriates but both, for the sake of their children, accepted that they had no real choice. Wentworth, epitomised by his generation as the Native Son, and Sarah, his currency lass, were doomed to wander through Europe like wealthy Gypsies, unable to plant new roots. Gum trees, wrote Sarah, cannot flourish in the snow. Wentworth had wanted Vaucluse maintained in their absence as a home for Sarah. He wanted her to have 'a home endeared to her ... by so many recollections'.[32] Ultimately both left their return home too late, ill health preventing them from enduring the long voyage back to Australia. In death, William returned but Sarah did not. Her remains were buried without a headstone in foreign soil, away from her beloved family and Vaucluse.

Notes

Abbreviations
ML   Mitchell Library, Sydney
NLA   National Library of Australia, Canberra
SLV   State Library of Victoria, Melbourne

Introduction
The arguments in this introduction draw generally upon Katrina Alford, *Production or Reproduction? An economic history of women in Australia 1788–1850*, Oxford University Press, Melbourne 1984, pp. 14–71; Alan Atkinson and Marian Aveling (eds), *Australians 1838*, Fairfax, Syme & Weldon, Sydney 1987, pp. 95–117; Leonore Davidoff and Catherine Hall, *Family Fortunes: Men and women of the English middle class, 1780–1850*, Hutchinson, London 1987; and Kay Schaffer, *Women and the Bush: Forces of desire in the Australian cultural tradition*, Cambridge University Press, Melbourne 1988.

[1] Wilson Hardy to Sarah Hardy, 22 March 1854, Wilson Hardy Collection, University of Melbourne Archives.
[2] Atkinson and Aveling, *Australians 1838*, p. 101.
[3] ibid.
[4] Wilson Hardy to Lizzie Hardy, 14 May 1860.
[5] Scott Family Papers, MS 38/79, ML.

John and Charlotte Bussell

[1] John Bussell's letter is printed as an appendix to E. O. G. Shann, *Cattle Chosen: The Story of the First Group Settlement in Western Australia 1829 to 1841*, (Oxford University Press 1926) University of Western Australia Press, 1978, pp. 147–57. The Bussells wrote Home—and later to each other in the colony—at length and often, and the family records deserve several years of some researcher's life. This piece limits itself to the published sources, and is only a preliminary exploration of the riches available. It is particularly dependent upon Shann's *Cattle Chosen* and the extracts and biographical material published by Ian D. Heppingstone and H. Margaret Wilson as ' "Mrs. John": The Letters of Charlotte Bussell of Cattle Chosen', in *Early Days* VII, 4–5, 1972–3.
[2] Shann, *Cattle Chosen*, p. 42.

[3] M. Aveling, Introduction to Shann's *Cattle Chosen*.
[4] Elizabeth Bussell to Frances Bussell, 5 November 1833, cited in Shann, *Cattle Chosen*, pp. 35–6.
[5] Leonore Davidoff and Catherine Hall, *Family Fortunes: Men and women of the English middle class, 1780–1850*, Hutchinson, London 1987, pp. 159–60.
[6] Shann describes John Bussell's library on p. 43. Davidoff and Hall discuss manly emotion and evangelical religion on pp. 110–11.
[7] Fanny Bussell reported to her mother that these qualities were more prevalent on the Swan than in England. Shann, *Cattle Chosen*, p. 33.
[8] ibid., p. 15.
[9] Davidoff and Hall, *Family Fortunes*, p. 110.
[10] The journal of the Reverend John Wollaston gives many examples of Bussell's ministry; see for example *Wollaston's Picton Journal 1841–1844*, ed. A. Burton and P. U. Henn, University of Western Australia Press, 1975, p. 31.
[11] G. C. Bolton, 'The idea of a colonial gentry', *Historical Studies*, 13, 1967–9, pp. 307–26.
[12] C. H. Manning Clark (*A History of Australia* vol. 3, Melbourne University Press, 1962–87, ch. 2) discusses the means and motives of the founding families of western Australia.
[13] J. G. A. Pocock, *Politics, Language and Time: Essays on Political Thought and History*, Methuen, London 1971, p. 110, citing J. Harrington's *Oceana*.
[14] Shann makes this point, and cites J. G. Bussell to Capel Carter, *Cattle Chosen*, p. 18.
[15] See ibid., p. 25.
[16] George Millar to Mrs Frances Bussell, undated, cited in ibid., p. 31.
[17] Fanny Bussell to Mrs Frances Bussell, undated, cited in ibid., p. 32.
[18] Fanny Bussell to Capel Carter, cited in ibid., p. 48.
[19] John Bussell to Capel Carter, 1836, cited in ibid., p. 92.
[20] ibid., p. 82.
[21] J. G. Bussell to Rev. C. Wells, Reeding Priory, 30 May 1832, cited in ibid., p. 72.
[22] Shann, citing Frances Bussell to Frances Louisa Bussell, March 1833, ibid., p. 33.
[23] ibid., p. 2.
[24] Frances Bussell to Capel Carter, early 1837?, cited in ibid., p. 42.
[25] Shann, citing an unnamed source, ibid., p. 129.
[26] Cited in ibid., p. 131.
[27] ibid., pp. 18, 130–1.
[28] Cited in ibid., p. 132.
[29] Cited in Heppingstone and Wilson, '"Mrs. John"', Part 1, p. 8.
[30] Cited in ibid., p. 9.
[31] See Davidoff and Hall, *Family Fortunes*, pp. 114–15.
[32] Heppingstone and Wilson, '"Mrs. John"', Part 1, p. 8.
[33] The entry on Brethren (Plymouth) in James Hastings (ed.) *Encyclopaedia of Religion and Ethics* vol. 2, Edinburgh 1901, pp. 843–7, gives a full account of the history and beliefs of the Plymouth Brethren, including some discussion of the peculiarities of the Providence Chapel under R. B. Newton in Charlotte's time. The quotations are taken from p. 847. Dorothy M. Valenze (*Prophetic Sons and Daughter: Female Preaching and Popular Religion in Industrial England*, Princeton University Press, New Jersey 1985) argues that the more humble the sect, the more readily it allowed women to speak. Charlotte comments in a much later letter about the Providence people's dislike of romantic literature, see Charlotte Bussell to ?, 5 November 1848, cited in Heppingstone and Wilson, '"Mrs. John"', Part 1, p. 24.
[34] John Bussell to unnamed correspondent, cited in Shann, *Cattle Chosen*, p. 133.
[35] Cited in Heppingstone and Wilson, '"Mrs. John"', Part 1, p. 9.
[36] John Bussell to Tom Arthur Bussell, March 1838, cited in ibid., p. 10.

Notes (Chapters 1 to 2) 137

[37] Charlotte Bussell to Fanny Bowker (?) June 1838 (?), cited in ibid., pp. 12–13.
[38] Charlotte Bussell to Fred and Mary Vines, 1883, cited in ibid., Part 2, p. 74.
[39] Fanny Bussell, 1833, cited in Shann, *Cattle Chosen*, p. 77.
[40] Fanny Bussell to Mrs Frances Bussell, 1833, cited in ibid., p. 33.
[41] Charles Bussell to John Bussell (of Henley), 1830?, cited in ibid., p. 23.
[42] Charlotte Bussell to Emily Bowker, August 1840, cited in Heppingstone and Wilson, '"Mrs. John"', Part 1, p. 15.
[43] Charlotte Bussell to Fanny Bowker, 1839, cited in ibid., p. 13.
[44] Charlotte Bussell to Mrs Emily Bowker, 25 July 1840, cited in ibid., pp. 14–15.
[45] Taken from 'A Typical Fortnight from Fanny Bussell's Diary. 7th to 20th June, 1840'. Shann, *Cattle Chosen*, Appendix 9, pp. 184–5.
[46] *Wollaston's Picton Journal 1841–1844*, Saturday 9 April 1842, p. 68.
[47] ibid., Friday 4 November 1842, p. 110.
[48] Charlotte Bussell to Emily Huggins, December 1840, cited in Heppingstone and Wilson, '"Mrs. John"', Part 1, p. 16.
[49] See Shann, *Cattle Chosen*, chs 7 and 8; the quotes are from pp. 121, 119.
[50] Charlotte Bussell, 1844, cited in Heppingstone and Wilson, '"Mrs. John"', Part 1, p. 21.
[51] ibid.
[52] Shann explains the 'colonial economy' of the Bussell enterprises in his chapter by that title, *Cattle Chosen*, ch. 6.
[53] ibid., p. 86.
[54] Charlotte Bussell, 1844, p. 21.
[55] It was held to be 'unbecoming' for Fanny to have to care for her invalid brother, Lennox, who had suffered a total mental and physical collapse under the terror of an anticipated Aboriginal attack. See Charles Bussell's plan for the operation of the estate, 1841, cited in Shann, *Cattle Chosen*, p. 138.
[56] See for example Charlotte Bussell to Fanny Bowker, 21 April 1842, cited in Heppingstone and Wilson, '"Mrs. John"', Part 1, pp. 18–21.
[57] Charlotte Bussell, 1848?, cited in ibid., p. 23.
[58] Charlotte Bussell, 17 February 1853, cited in ibid., p. 27.
[59] Charlotte Bussell to Fanny Bussell (née Bowker, now married to Tom Arthur Bussell), 20 July 1855, cited in ibid., Part 2, p. 44.
[60] Charlotte Bussell to John Garrett Bussell, 1 September 1858, included as Appendix 8 in Shann, *Cattle Chosen*, pp. 179–84; this quote from p. 181.
[61] *Wollaston's Picton Journal*, Sunday 25 September 1842, p. 104.
[62] Bishop Hale, cited in Heppingstone and Wilson, '"Mrs. John"', Part 2, p. 55.
[63] Charlotte Bussell to John Garrett Bussell, 5 April 1864, cited in ibid., p. 55.
[64] Charlotte Bussell to John Garret Bussell, April 1864, cited in ibid., p. 56.
[65] John Bussell to Charlotte Bussell, May 1864, cited in ibid., p. 56.
[66] Charlotte Bussell to John Spicer, 1871?, cited in ibid., p. 63.
[67] Mary Yates, née Bussell, cited in ibid., p. 67
[68] Charlotte Bussell to Alfred Bussell, October 1877, cited in ibid., p. 68.
[69] Charlotte Bussell to Capel Brockman, née Bussell, ?1884, cited in ibid., p. 74.
[70] Davidoff and Hall, *Family Fortunes*, ch. 7.

Elizabeth and John Macarthur

[1] Bridgerule Baptismal Register, 1766; Land Tax Assessments, Bridgerule, 1780–89, Devon County Record Office, Exeter; Elizabeth Macarthur to her son Edward, 3 June 1844, 14 August 1846, vol. 11, Macarthur Papers. (Future references MP followed by volume number.) For further information about Elizabeth Macarthur and her family and a detailed bibliography see Hazel King, *Elizabeth Macarthur and her*

World, Sydney University Press, 1980, and *Colonial Expatriates: Edward and John Macarthur Junior*, Kangaroo Press, Kenthurst 1989.
[2] Bridget Kingdon to Elizabeth Macarthur, 15 September 1799, MP 10; *Alumni Oxonienses 1715–1888*, London, 1888, p. 139.
[3] Bailey's *Western & Midland Directory*, 1783; Stoke Damerel Baptisms and Burials 1759–86, West Devon County Record Office, Plymouth; Elizabeth Macarthur to Eliza Kingdon, March 1816, James Macarthur to Roger Therry, 24 February 1859, MP 1, 2; *Annual Lists of Officers in the Army*, 1783, 1784.
[4] Bridgerule Parish Registers, Baptisms and Marriages, 1788; Elizabeth Macarthur to her mother, 20 April 1790; Edward Macarthur to his mother, November 1809; Elizabeth Macarthur jnr to her brother Edward, 18 March 1841, MP 12, 16, 17; *List of Officers*, London 1789; William Blackstone, *Commentaries on the Laws of England*, vol. 1, London 1825.
[5] Elizabeth Macarthur to Bridget Kingdon, 1 September [1798?]; to her mother, 8 October 1789, MP 12.
[6] Elizabeth Macarthur's Journal of her voyage to New South Wales, MP 10.
[7] ibid.
[8] Elizabeth Macarthur to her mother, 20 April 1790, 18 March 1791, MP 12.
[9] Elizabeth Macarthur to her mother, 18 March 1791, MP 12.
[10] Elizabeth Macarthur to Bridget Kingdon, 7 March 1791, 1 September [1798?], MP 10, 12; *List of Officers*, 1797.
[11] Elizabeth Macarthur to John Piper, 15 April 1804, Piper Papers, Mitchell Library, Sydney.
[12] ibid.
[13] Elizabeth Macarthur to Garnham Blaxcell, 30 May 1809, MP 10.
[14] Elizabeth Macarthur to Eliza Kingdon, March 1816, MP 12; Returns of Sheep and Cattle, MP 103.
[15] Macarthur to Elizabeth, 8 December 1814, 3 August 1810, MP 2.
[16] Elizabeth Macarthur to Eliza Kingdon, 11 December 1817, 6 February 1825, MP 12.
[17] Elizabeth Macarthur to her son Edward, 3 July 1832, MP 10.
[18] ibid., 17 May 1834, MP 10.
[19] Will of John Macarthur, signed 11 April 1828, NSW Registrar in Probate, Wills, Series I, No. 613.
[20] Elizabeth Macarthur to her son Edward, 12 October 1842, MP 11.

Sir John and Lady Jane Franklin

Note: Precise dates for letters and diaries are often not available.
[1] Jane Franklin to John Franklin, 1832, in Frances J. Woodward, *Portrait of Jane: A Life of Lady Franklin*, Hodder & Stoughton, London 1951, p. 182.
[2] Jane Franklin to Mary Simpkinson, 13 February 1839, Archives Office of Tasmania, NS 279/2.
[3] Diary, 1821, in Woodward, *Portrait*, p. 115.
[4] Diary, 1819, in ibid., pp. 97, 115.
[5] Diary, n.d., in ibid., p. 134.
[6] 'A Plan for the employment of time etc.', April 1811, in ibid. pp. 19–21.
[7] Kathleen Fitzpatrick, *Sir John Franklin in Tasmania, 1837–1843*, Melbourne University Press, 1949, pp. 33–4.
[8] ibid., pp. 33–7.
[9] Woodward, *Portrait*, pp. 156–9.
[10] Jane Griffin to John Franklin, 1828, in Fitzpatrick, *Sir John Franklin*, pp. 40–1.
[11] Jane Franklin to John Franklin, December 1830, in Woodward, *Portrait*, p. 163.
[12] Jane Franklin to John Franklin, March 1831, in ibid., p. 169.

Notes (Chapters 3 to 4) 139

[13] Jane Franklin to John Franklin, n.d., in ibid., pp. 168, 170.
[14] John Franklin to Jane Franklin, 1834, in ibid., p. 191.
[15] In 1840 they saw this wish come true, but there was a sting in its tail. The British government ended transportation to New South Wales in 1840, continuing it to Norfolk Island and Tasmania and destroying at a blow Franklin's hopes for representative government for the colony and the encouragement of free settlers who would improve the character of society. But at the same they ended the assignment system which the landholders relied on for cheap labour, and which was their main reason for demanding the continuance of transportation to the colony. See Fitzpatrick, *Sir John Franklin*, pp. 222–37.
[16] See ibid., pp. 134–7.
[17] Jane Franklin to Mary Simpkinson, 1838, in ibid., pp. 130–1.
[18] ibid., p. 128.
[19] John Franklin to James Clark Ross, 13 September 1842, in ibid., p. 260.
[20] Jane Franklin to Henslowe, n.d., in ibid., p. 129.
[21] Jane Franklin to Mary Simpkinson, 1838, in ibid., p. 131.
[22] Woodward, *Portrait*, p. 208.
[23] Fitzpatrick, *Sir John Franklin*, p. 81; Jane Franklin to Mary Simpkinson, n.d., in Woodward, *Portrait*, p. 217.
[24] Mrs Machonochie to Sir George Back, 1839, in ibid., p. 208.
[25] Montagu's 'Book', cited in Fitzpatrick, *Sir John Franklin*, p. 351.
[26] ibid., p. 131.
[27] Jane Franklin to Mary Simpkinson, 10 September 1842, in ibid., p. 260.
[28] Jane Franklin to James Clark Ross, 3 April 1842, in ibid., p. 271.
[29] Jane Franklin to Mary Simpkinson, 6 November 1841, in ibid., p. 264.
[30] [Sir John Franklin] *Narrative of some passages in the history of Van Diemen's Land, during the last three years of Sir John Franklin's administration of its government*, Platypus Publications, Hobart 1967, pp. 27–8; Fitzpatrick, *Sir John Franklin*, pp. 266–7, 275.
[31] Franklin, *Narrative*, p. 20.
[32] John Montagu to Dr Turnbull, Memorandum, 11 September 1844, included in Franklin, *Narrative*, pp. 133–4.
[33] Dr Turnbull to John Montagu, 11 September 1844, included in Franklin, *Narrative*, p. 138.
[34] Montagu's 'Book', cited in Fitzpatrick, *Sir John Franklin*, p. 357.
[35] ibid., p. 373.
[36] Woodward, *Portrait*, pp. 250–1.
[37] Franklin, *Narrative*, pp. 28–9.
[38] Letter from J. E. Bicheno to ?, 1845, cited in Alison Alexander, *Governors' Ladies: The Wives and Mistresses of Van Diemen's Land Governors* Tasmanian Historical Research Association, 1987, p. 120.

Charles and Sophie La Trobe

[1] *The Rambler in North America* vol. 1, R. B. Seeley and W. Burnside, London 1836, p. 4.
[2] ibid., p. 7. For La Trobe's early life and information on the La Trobe, de Montmollin and Pourtalès families, see Jill Eastwood, 'La Trobe, Charles Joseph', in A. G. L. Shaw and C. M. H. Clark (eds), *Australian Dictionary of Biography*, vol. 2, Melbourne University Press, 1967; Jill Eastwood, *Charles Joseph La Trobe*, Oxford University Press, Melbourne 1972; Jacques Petitpierre, 'Les Deux Hymens Neuchâteloise du Premier Gouverneur de l'État de Victoria' in *Patrie Neuchâteloise*, vol. 4, Éditions H. Messeiller, Neuchâtel 1955.
[3] *The Alpenstock; or, Sketches of Swiss Scenery and Manners 1825–1826*, R. B. Seeley and W. Burnside, London 1829, p. 3.

140   Notes (Chapter 4)

[4] *The Pedestrian: a Summer's Ramble in the Tyrol, and Some of the Adjacent Provinces, 1830*, R. B. Seeley and W. Burnside, London 1832, p. 13.
[5] 'Journal & c 1829–1830 No. I', La Trobe Archive, La Trobe Collection, SLV.
[6] *A Tour of the Prairies*, quoted in Alan Gross, *Charles Joseph La Trobe*, Melbourne University Press, 1956, p. 7.
[7] MS 12488, 'Private Memoranda. New Series from my return to England July 1834 to Sept 1836'; marriage certificate, Archives Jacques Petitpierre, Archives de l'État, Neuchâtel, Switzerland.
[8] Fragment of a letter, 20 March 1837, Archives Jacques Petitpierre.
[9] 'New South Wales Diary & c 1839', ibid.
[10] A. G. L. Shaw (ed.), *Gipps-La Trobe Correspondence 1839–1846*, Melbourne University Press, 1989, pp. 6, 11–15, 24, 28–33, 164; Sally Graham, *Pioneer Merchant: the Letters of James Graham, 1939–54*, Hyland House, South Yarra, Vic. 1985, pp. 67–8.
[11] Shaw, *Gipps-La Trobe Correspondence*, pp. 34–6.
[12] ibid., p. 40.
[13] MS 7662, 2 March 1840, La Trobe Papers.
[14] ibid. For Jolimont, see Miles Lewis, 'Jolimont Melbourne' in Australian Council of National Trusts, *Historic Houses*, combined edn, Heritage Reprints, Canberra 1982, pp. 86–93; *Victoria's First Government House 1839-1854*, 6th edn, National Trust of Australia (Victoria), Melbourne 1987; for Charlotte Pellet, see Joan M. Ritchie, 'Housekeeper of Jolimont: a Biographical Sketch of Charlotte Pellet (1800–76)', *Victorian Historical Journal* 47, November 1976, pp. 277–83.
[15] Quoted in Samuel Smiles, *A Publisher and his Friends* vol. 2, John Murray, London 1891, p. 457.
[16] C. J. La Trobe to R. C. Gunn, 17 August 1848. Quoted in L. J. Blake (ed.), *Letters of Charles Joseph La Trobe*, Government of Victoria, Melbourne 1975, p. 32.
[17] MS 000026, Robert Williams Pohlman, Diary, 21 October 1840, 19 December 1840, Royal Historical Society of Victoria. For the La Trobes' social circle in Melbourne, see Paul de Serville, *Port Phillip Gentlemen and Good Society in Melbourne before the Gold Rushes*, Oxford University Press, Melbourne 1980, pp. 55–8
[18] Georgiana McCrae, Journal, 18 April 1845, Chaplin Collection, Fisher Library, University of Sydney.
[19] MS 12018, Georgiana McCrae, Journal, 18 March 1841, McCrae Family Papers, La Trobe Collection, SLV; 17 November 1850, Chaplin Collection.
[20] Quoted in Smiles, *A Publisher and his Friends* vol. 2, p. 457.
[21] H15609, La Trobe Papers.
[22] MS PA88/7, Sophie La Trobe to Susan Norton, 15 September 1848, Norton Family Papers, La Trobe Collection, SLV
[23] Georgiana McCrae, Journal, 16 November 1850, Chaplin Collection.
[24] 13 August 1853, quoted in Blake, *Letters*, p. 42.
[25] H15613, 19 March 1848, La Trobe Papers.
[26] H15615 [September 1848], La Trobe Papers.
[27] MS 15604 'Memoranda of Journeys, Excursions & Absences—Port Phillip & Victoria 1839–1854', pp. 221, 283, 237, La Trobe Papers.
[28] MS 000317, C. J. La Trobe to Julia Latrobe, 8 June 1842, photocopy of holograph, Royal Historical Society of Victoria.
[29] Shaw, *Gipps-La Trobe Correspondence*, pp. 327 and 365.
[30] 16 February 1846, Archives Jacques Petitpierre.
[31] 28 February 1851, ibid.
[32] MS H15619, 28 October 1853, La Trobe Papers.
[33] Quoted in Graham, *Pioneer Merchant*, p. 243.
[34] C. J. La Trobe to Julia Latrobe, Royal Historical Society of Victoria.
[35] C. J. La Trobe to D. C. McArthur, 27 July [1855], quoted in Blake, *Letters*, p. 50.

Notes (Chapters 5 to 6) 141

Caroline and Archibald Chisholm

[1] The sources for much of the biographical material in this chapter are: Caroline Chisholm, *Female Immigration Considered in a Brief Account of the Sydney Immigrants' Home*, London 1842; Eneas Mackenzie, *Memoirs of Mrs. Chisholm with an Account of her Philanthropic Labours in India, Australia and England*; Margaret Kiddle, *Caroline Chisholm*, Melbourne 1950; Mary Hoban, *Fifty-one Pieces of Wedding Cake: A Biography of Caroline Chisholm*, Kilmore, Vic. 1973. Mary Hoban in particular went to enormous efforts to trace extant material on or by the Chisholms, and this essay owes much to her painstaking detailed work.
[2] Mackenzie, *Memoirs*, pp. 3–4.
[3] A Lady (Lady Julia Charlotte Maitland), *Letters from Madras During the Years 1836–1839*, London 1843, cited Hoban, *Fifty-one Pieces of Wedding Cake*, p. 14.
[4] *Cork Examiner*, 1852, cited Hoban, ibid., p. 286.
[5] Chisholm, *Female Immigration Considered*, pp. 2–4.
[6] Hoban, *Fifty-one Pieces of Wedding Cake*, p. 94.
[7] *Sidney's Emigrants' Journal*, 1850, cited Kiddle, *Caroline Chisholm*, p. 14.
[8] Chisholm, *Female Immigration Considered*, p. 10.
[9] ibid., p. 57.
[10] ibid., p. 12.
[11] Roger Therry, *Reminiscences of Thirty Years' Residence in New South Wales and Victoria*, 1863, cited Hoban, *Fifty-one Pieces of Wedding Cake*, p. 84.
[12] *Sydney Morning Herald*, 18 January 1844, cited ibid., p. 127.
[13] Thomas Callaghan, 'The Diary of Thomas Callaghan', *RAHS Journal*, 1948, cited ibid., pp. 81–2.
[14] Caroline Chisholm, *Prospectus of a Work to be Entitled 'Voluntary Information from the People of New South Wales . . .'*, Sydney 1845.
[15] Caroline Chisholm, *Emigration and Transportation Relatively Considered*, London 1847.
[16] *Sydney Morning Herald*, 5 April 1847, cited Kiddle, *Caroline Chisholm*, p. 95.
[17] Mackenzie, *Memoirs*.
[18] Hoban, *Fifty-one Pieces of Wedding Cake*, p. 266.
[19] ibid., p. 240.
[20] MacKenzie, *Memoirs*, p. 144.
[21] *Sydney Morning Herald*, 22 February 1861, cited Hoban, *Fifty-one Pieces of Wedding Cake*, p. 400.
[22] *Times*, 16 August 1852, cited ibid., p. 290.
[23] *Argus*, 1 July 1852, cited ibid., p. 277.
[24] *Bendigo Advertiser*, 27 November 1854, cited ibid., p. 392.
[25] *Empire*, 13 June 1862, cited ibid., p. 403.
[26] *Sydney Morning Herald*, [10] July 1859, cited ibid., p. 392.
[27] Monica Gruggan to J. F. Thomas, 27 January 1925, ML, cited ibid., p. 414.
[28] *Sydney Morning Herald*, 26 January 1924, (article by E. Dwyer-Grey), cited ibid., p. 295.

Sarah and William Wentworth

[1] Carol Liston, *Sarah Wentworth, Mistress of Vaucluse*, Historic Houses Trust, Sydney 1988, pp. 13, 17. This essay is based on *Sarah Wentworth*. Research material for the book was provided by the Historic Houses Trust and transcripts of the original materials are held in the Trust's library at Lyndhurst, Glebe.
[2] A. Macleay to J. Deas Thomson, 8 July 1829 quoted in S. G. Foster, *Colonial Improver: Edward Dead Thomson 1800–1879* Melbourne University Press, 1978, p. 21.
[3] *Australian*, 23 September 1829.

Notes (Chapter 6)

4. *Sydney Morning Herald*, 9 February 1843.
5. Liston, *Sarah Wentworth*, pp. 33–6.
6. A. Summers, *Damned Whores and God's Police*, Penguin, Harmondsworth 1975, p. 296.
7. E. Darling to A. Dumaresq, 13 December 1832, ML MSS 2566.
8. Lady Franklin, 'Journal of a journey from Port Phillip to Sydney 1839', NLA MS 114.
9. Eliza Wentworth to Thomasine Fisher, 13 February 1844, ML A868.
10. Callaghan Diary, 23 July 1844, ML A2112/1, p.157; Liston, *Sarah Wentworth*, pp. 43–6, 91–2.
11. Wentworth to Willie, 7 September 1844, ML A756, p. 219.
12. Eliza Wentworth to Thomasine Fisher, n.d. (1844), ML A868.
13. Elizabeth Macarthur to Edward Macarthur, 3 June 1847, ML A2907.
14. G. C. Mundy, *Our Antipodes: or Residence and Rambles in the Australasian Colonies*, Richard Bentley, London 1852, vol. 1, pp. 371–2.
15. *Sydney Morning Herald*, 27 May 1847.
16. Liston, *Sarah Wentworth*, p. 54.
17. Sarah Wentworth to Thomasine Fisher, 3 May 1854, ML 868.
18. ibid.
19. Liston, *Sarah Wentworth*, p. 64.
20. ibid., p. 63.
21. ibid., p. 80
22. James Macarthur to Emily Macarthur, (27?) September 1852 (private collection).
23. *People's Advocate*, 25 August 1849.
24. W. C. Wentworth to James Macarthur, 3 April 1854, ML A2923, p. 217.
25. Sarah Wentworth to Fisher, 31 December 1868, ML A868.
26. Liston, *Sarah Wentworth*, pp. 98–100.
27. ibid., pp. 88–90.
28. ibid., pp. 95–8.
29. Lucy Wentworth to Thomasine Fisher, 20 September 1873, ML A868.
30. Liston, *Sarah Wentworth*, pp. 105–13.
31. ibid., p. 101.
32. ibid., p. 100.

Index

Compiled by Russell Brooks

Aborigines, 13, 25, 45, 87, 109
Argo, 42
Arthur, Governor George, 59, 60, 61, 64
Atlas, 125
Australian, 118

Bendigo Advertiser, 112
Bligh, Governor, 43
Bourke, Governor, 121, 122
Bowker, John and Emily, 20, 24
Bowman, James, 47
Bowman, Lucy, 133
Broadhurst, Edward, 126
Buchan, Captain David, 54
Bussell, Charlotte
  children, 20, 21, 25, 26, 30
  death, 30
  letters, 22–3, 24, 26, 27, 28, 30
  management skills, 4, 25–6, 27
  marriage, 3, 10, 20
Bussell, Fanny, 18, 19, 23, 24, 25
Bussell, John Garrett
  character, 15–19
  children, 25, 26
  death, 30
  education, 16
  letters, 12, 14–15, 22, 28
  marriage, 3, 4, 10, 20
  political career, 27
Butini, Adolphe, 52

Callaghan, Thomas, 108
Camden, Lord, 42
Campbell, Robert, 115
Carter, Capel, 19
Cattle Chosen, 23, 24, 27, 30
children
  and education, 39, 40, 42, 43, 90, 99–100, 102, 115, 127, 128
  in the colonies, 26, 89, 90, 103, 104, 106, 115
  see also women
Chisholm, Archibald
  children, 99–100, 101, 106, 107, 110
  death, 113
  marriage, 4, 94, 96, 98, 100, 102, 108–9, 111
  military career, 10, 94, 97, 98, 100, 101, 102, 108, 112
Chisholm, Caroline (mother)
  character, 111
  childhood, 94–6
  children, 99–100, 101, 106, 107, 110
  death, 113
  Madras school, 98–100
  marriage, 4, 94, 96, 98, 100, 102, 108–9, 111
  on colonial policy, 105, 109
  social conscience, 95–9, 102–13
Chisholm, Caroline (daughter), 110
Chisholm, Henry, 102, 106
Chisholm, Monica, 110, 113

143

144 Index

Chisholm, Sydney, 110
Chisholm, William, 100
colonial life *see* children, marriage, morality, women colonial society, 2–11, 17, 18, 24, 37–9, 52, 59, 61, 63–9, 83–6, 99, 102–4, 105–7, 109, 115, 118, 120–6, 128, 133
Constitution Bill, 127
convict
 labour, 26, 40, 41, 42, 45
 transportation, 35–6, 60, 61, 65, 116
 Parramatta uprising, 40–1
convicts, female, 36, 38, 63–4, 94–113
Cooksworthy, Charlotte *see* Bussell, Charlotte
Cox, Francis, 116, 132
Cox, Sarah *see* Wentworth, Sarah
Crowley, Catherine, 115

Dana, Captain Henry Pulteney, 87
Darling, Eliza, 121
Darling, Governor, 128
de Montmollin, Sophie *see* La Trobe, Sophie
Derwent Bank, 59
Dickens, Charles, 111
Dunbar, Rev Charles, 133

Elizabeth Farm, 38, 44, 47, 48, 49, 115
Emerald Isle, 101

Family Colonization Loan Society, 110, 112
Female Immigrants' Home, 113
female immigration, 102–4, 105–6, 107–9, 110–11
Fisher, Thomas John, 122
Fisher, Willie, 132
Fitzpatrick, Kathleen, 54, 56
FitzRoy, Governor, 122
Fitzwilliam, Earl, 115
Flinders, Matthew, 54
Franklin, Eleanor (daughter), 57
Franklin, Lady Jane
 exploration, 10, 57, 58, 59, 78
 health, 58
 letters, 50, 56–7, 62, 66
 marriage, 3, 5, 51, 52–4, 56, 57, 58, 62
 on colonial policy, 50, 51–2, 59, 61–3, 65–6, 68–9
 opinion of Sarah Wentworth, 121

Franklin, Sir John
 and the 'Arthur faction', 59, 60, 61
 Arctic exploration, 6, 51, 54, 55–6, 69, 70, 72
 as Lieutenant-Governor, 3, 50, 58, 59, 60–1, 64, 69
 children, 57
 death, 71–2
 letters, 61–2
 marriage, 54, 56, 57, 58

Gipps, Lady, 105, 122
Gipps, Sir George, 78, 79, 81, 90, 104, 105
Graham, James, 81, 92
Grey, Earl, 109
Griffin, Jane *see* Franklin, Lady Jane
Grose, Major, 33, 39
Gunn, Ronald Campbell, 87

Hardy, Polly, 8
Hardy, Wilson, 6, 7–8
Hatherley, John, 31
Haywood, Sophie, 19–20
Herbert, Thomas, 45
Hill, Mary Jane, 132
Hoban, Mary, 104

immigration *see* female immigration
Irving, Washington, 75

Jones, Caroline *see* Chisolm, Caroline

Keays-Young, Captain Henry, 133
King, Governor, 39–40, 42–3
Kingdon, Rev John, 31

La Trobe, Agnes Louisa, 77, 89–90, 91
La Trobe, Cecile, 86
La Trobe, Charles, 86
La Trobe, Charles Joseph
 as Lieutenant-Governor, 79–81, 91
 as Superintendent, 78, 79, 81, 84
 character, 73, 83–4
 children, 77, 86, 89
 death, 93
 expeditions, 77, 87
 letters, 77–8, 79, 83, 88, 91
 marriage, 2, 73, 74, 77, 81, 92
 publications, 75, 76, 77
La Trobe, Eleanora (Nelly), 86
La Trobe, Sophie

children, 77, 86, 89
death, 92
health, 73, 78, 86–7, 88
letters, 91
marriage, 3, 4, 5, 73, 74, 77
land
relationship to men, 3, 16–17, 40
Lonsdale, Captain William, 79
Lord Eldon, 46
Lord, Simeon, 116
Lucas, Penelope, 42, 43, 47

Macarthur, Edward, 33, 36, 37, 39, 42, 46, 47, 49
Macarthur, Elizabeth (daughter), 38, 40, 42, 43, 49
Macarthur, Elizabeth (mother)
children, 33, 35, 36–7, 38, 39, 40, 42, 43, 118
death, 49
education, 32
letters, 33–4, 35, 36, 37, 39, 40, 41, 43, 45, 46, 47, 49, 124
management skills, 4, 39, 40, 43–4, 45, 46–7, 49
marriage, 3, 10, 31, 32–3, 34, 47, 49
Macarthur, Emmeline, 43
Macarthur, Hannibal, 42, 43
Macarthur, James (the second), 39, 43, 46, 48, 129–30
Macarthur, John (father)
army career, 32, 33, 38, 39, 41
character, 3, 35, 38, 39, 43, 47
children, 33, 35, 36–7, 38, 39, 40, 42, 43, 118
death, 49
education, 32
health, 36, 37, 47
land grant, 42–3, 44–5, 46
letters, 45–6
marriage, 3, 10, 31, 32–3, 34, 47, 49
relationship with Wentworth, 118
'Rum Rebellion', 43, 46
Macarthur, John (son), 38, 40, 42, 47
Macarthur, Mary, 38, 47
Macarthur, William, 39, 43, 46, 48
McCrae, Georgiana, 85, 86, 87
MacKenzie, Eneas, 111, 112
McNeal, Ann Lawes, 116, 122
Maconochie, Alexander, 61, 64
Macquarie, Governor, 43, 44
Maitland, Lady Julia, 98

marriage
and domesticity, 3, 7, 8, 23
and sexuality, 3, 99, 105
in the colonies, 1–11, 30, 73, 104–5, 107–8, 109, 115, 116–18, 122–4, 126, 129, 130, 134
selection of partners, 4, 6–8, 20, 23, 30, 105, 107–8, 115
Mitchell, Mrs, 8–9
Montagu, John, 50, 52, 59, 64, 65, 66–8, 70
morality in the colonies, 7, 18, 102–5, 109, 113, 115, 118, 120–1, 125, 126, 132
see also women
More, Hannah, 95
Morton, Fanny, 116
Murray, John, 83, 86

names
public and private use of, 5
Neptune, 35, 36

Paterson, Colonel, 39
Payne, John, 116–17
Pellet, Charlotte, 83, 91
Phillip, Governor, 38
Plymouth Brethren, 21
poetry, 8–9
Pohlmans, Robert Williams, 84–5
Porden, Eleanor, 54, 55–6

Rajah, 90
Reibey, Mary, 116
Reilly, Anne, 133
religion, 21–2, 95–6
Roget, Dr Peter Mark, 52
'Rum Rebellion', 43

Scarborough, 35, 36
Scott, Harriet, 126
Scotts (family), 8
Second fleet, 35–6, 37
Shann, Edward, 15, 19, 25
Sidney, Samuel, 111
social
classes, 7–8, 17, 18, 103, 107, 115, 125–6
reform, 95–6, 112
status, 18, 23, 84, 107, 118, 122, 124–6, 128, 130
society *see* colonial society

Index

Stanley, Lord James, 68, 69
Surprise, 35
Swan River Colony, 16, 17, 18, 21
Sydney Morning Herald, 107, 125

Therry, Roger, 107, 108
Todhunter, Elizabeth, 115
Turnbull, Dr, 67, 68

Vaucluse House, 114–15, 117, 120, 121, 134
Veale, Elizabeth *see* Macarthur, Elizabeth

Wardell, Robert, 122
Wentworth, D'Arcy (father), 115, 116, 122, 127
Wentworth, D'Arcy (son), 128, 133
Wentworth, Major D'Arcy, 122
Wentworth, Edith, 133
Wentworth, Eliza (Didy), 133
Wentworth, Eliza McPherson, 122, 123
Wentworth, Fanny, 123, 128, 132
Wentworth, Fitzwilliam, 120, 126, 127, 128, 132
Wentworth, Isabelle, 128
Wentworth, Laura, 133
Wentworth, Sarah, 4–5, 7, 10
　character, 7, 116, 119, 120–1, 125–6, 128, 129–30, 132
　children, 120, 122–5, 126–7, 128, 132
　death, 129, 132
　health, 119, 120
　management skills, 130–2
　marriage, 4–5, 7, 115, 118, 128, 130, 132, 134
Wentworth, Sarah (Joody), 128
Wentworth, Thomasine, 117, 122–3, 132
Wentworth, William Charles
　character, 4–5, 10, 117, 118, 120, 130, 133
　children, 118, 120, 126–7, 128, 132
　death, 129, 133
　education, 115
　health, 130–2
　letters, 129
　marriage, 4–5, 7, 115, 118, 128, 130, 132, 134
　political career, 121, 122, 123, 125, 126, 127, 128, 129, 130
Wentworth, William Charles (Willie), 117, 126–7, 128
Wilberforce, William, 95
Willis, Mrs, 79
women
　and morality, 103, 105, 113, 115, 120–1, 125, 127, 132
　as farm managers, 4, 25, 26–7, 28, 40, 43–7, 132
　in the colonies, 6–7, 9–10, 23–4, 26, 37–40, 43, 44, 45–6, 49, 50, 52, 63–70, 84–6, 88, 102–9, 112–3, 120–2, 125, 128
　separation from children, 9, 10, 26, 30, 31, 53, 39, 40, 43, 46, 89, 90, 106, 115, 122, 126
women's labour, 23, 26, 103
wool, 40, 41–2, 45, 115